Held
Daily Reflections for Living Gently

Vanessa France

Grace & Light Press

Copyright © 2026 by Vanessa France
All rights reserved.

No part of this book may be reproduced, stored in a retrieval system, or transmitted in any form or by any means – electronic, mechanical, photocopying, recording, or otherwise – without prior written permission from the publisher or author, except as permitted by U.S. copyright law.

The reflections in this book are offered for inspirational purposes only and are not intended as medical, psychological, or therapeutic advice.

Cover spread photography by Kaeli Rasmussen, taken at our beautiful VT camp on Lake Champlain.

Published by Grace & Light Press

ISBN (paperback): 979-8-9930743-4-4
ISBN (ebook): 979-8-9930743-5-1

Printed in the United States of America
First edition

Table of Contents

Preface	IV
1. January	1
2. February	33
3. March	62
4. April	94
5. May	125
6. June	157
7. July	188
8. August	220
9. September	252
10. October	283
11. November	315
12. December	346
Closing	379

Preface

This book was shaped quietly, long before I began writing it.

During my early years of sobriety, I was rarely without the voices that taught me how to live one day at a time. Melody Beattie and Mark Nepo became steady companions – not as answers, but as presence. Their words reminded me that reflection did not have to be complicated, that honesty mattered more than insight, and that healing often happens quietly, one ordinary day at a time.

Their books went everywhere with me. Pages softened with use. Spines bent and frayed from being carried through early mornings, between responsibilities, in parked cars before teaching class, and in the quiet hours when the house was still asleep. They were books I lived with.

In the year after I finished writing *Unraveled* – my memoir about healing, sobriety, and learning how to live honestly inside my own life – I found myself returning to my journal, jotting things down wherever I was, often in the notes app on my phone. Not to explain the past, but to notice what was still unfolding after the breaking open.

Many of these reflections were written for my yoga students, often just before a class or after a shared moment in the room, offered not as instruction but as something to carry – onto the mat, into the body, and into life. Shaped by the seasons of New England, these pages reflect winters of endurance and deep rest, springs of tenderness and hope, summers of warmth and movement, and falls of reflection and letting go. Some entries were written at home, others while traveling, in between responsibilities and moments of learning, coping, falling apart, and coming back together again. None of it tidy. All of it honest.

This book is meant to be lived with. You might open it in the quiet of the morning, read a page before bed and let it settle, or return to a single reflection again and again. You might share one aloud at the end of a class or gathering. There is no right way to hold it. You don't have to read it in order, or arrive feeling healed or certain or ready. You only need to meet the page you're on.

My hope is that somewhere in these words, you feel held – by the rhythm of the year, by the shared human experience of becoming, and by the quiet knowing that none of us do this alone.

With love,
Vanessa

January

A beginning that asks for gentleness, not certainty.

January 1st: A Quiet Beginning

A beginning does not always arrive with energy or clarity. Sometimes it comes quietly, while you are still tired and unsure, simply as you are.

There is a subtle pressure at the start of a year to feel ready. To wake up with direction and resolve that matches the date on the calendar. But real beginnings rarely feel like that. More often, they unfold gently, almost unnoticed, while life continues exactly as it is.

Some beginnings look like staying seated a moment longer before standing.
Like holding a warm mug and letting the quiet linger.
Like admitting you don't know what comes next and choosing not to rush yourself toward an answer.
Like allowing honesty to matter more than ambition, and presence more than performance.

This day does not need to be inspired or impressive.
It does not need to prove anything.
It only needs to be real.

Today, let yourself begin gently. Let life meet you exactly where you are – already held.

January 2nd: Winter Energy

There are seasons when the earth rests.
Trees stand bare. Fields lie quiet. Growth pulls inward, hidden from view.

Nothing in nature apologizes for this pause. Nothing rushes toward bloom before it is ready.

And yet, in those same seasons, we often expect ourselves to do the opposite. To wake up energized and focused. To move forward with clarity and momentum, even when our bodies feel heavy and our hearts are still carrying the weight of everything they've lived through.

Winter energy holds a different kind of wisdom. It reminds us that rest is not laziness or failure. It is part of the cycle. It is how strength rebuilds quietly, beneath the surface, where no one is watching and nothing needs to be explained.

This stillness is not empty. It is working in ways you cannot see.

Nothing is wasted here. Nothing is falling behind.

Today, notice one place where you can soften your pace. Trust that this gentler rhythm is not only enough, but necessary.

January 3rd: You Don't Have to Know Yet

Sometimes the greatest relief is realizing you do not have to know yet.
Not what's next.
Not how it will all work out.
Not who you are supposed to become.

There can be deep relief in allowing uncertainty to exist without rushing to resolve it. Space opens where pressure used to live. The effort of figuring everything out loosens, and you remember that life does not reveal itself all at once.

Not knowing is not a failure of clarity or courage. It is often an invitation – to listen more closely, to stay present, to allow understanding to take shape slowly instead of forcing it into form.

You are allowed to pause here.
You are allowed to rest without urgency.

Today, let yourself live inside the unknown rather than trying to solve it. Let not knowing become a place where you can breathe.

January 4th: Morning Light

Morning light does not ask whether you are ready for the day. It arrives anyway, slipping quietly across floors and countertops, catching on windows, stretching gently into the room before you've fully opened your eyes.

There is something kind about this. Light does not wait for clarity or motivation. It does not require you to feel inspired. It simply shows up, offering a small beginning without expectation.

You don't have to change anything about yourself to receive it. You don't have to fix the day before it starts. Sometimes the most honest way to begin is simply to notice what is already here.

Today, notice where the light lands first. Let it be enough to remind you that something is always quietly starting again.

January 5th: The Body Knows

Your body carries wisdom older than your plans. Older than your goals. Older than the expectations you've learned to place on yourself.

It knows when it's tired. It knows when it needs warmth, nourishment, stillness, or space. It notices long before your mind is willing to admit it.

So often, we override these signals. We push through discomfort. We talk ourselves out of rest. We treat the body like something to manage instead of something to listen to. Productivity and expectation grow louder, and the body's quiet language gets ignored.

But your body has never stopped communicating. It has been adapting, protecting, and carrying you through everything you've lived.

You do not need to push to be worthy.
You do not need to earn rest.
Your body is not asking for perfection. It is asking for care.

Today, pause long enough to ask your body what it needs. See if you can honor one small request without negotiating it away.

January 6th: Let What's Next Come to You

You don't need to chase what comes next.
You don't need to force direction, meaning, or certainty into place.

Some things arrive quietly. Gradually. Almost without notice. A small easing. A little more space. A sense of possibility you don't quite trust yet.

So much of life unfolds this way. Not through urgency, but through patience. Not through effort alone, but through allowing time to do its work. What is meant to meet you does not require pursuit.

Growth does not always ask for momentum. Sometimes it asks for room.

Today, practice letting what's next approach you instead of reaching toward it. Stay where you are. Trust that what belongs to you will find its way, without being rushed.

January 7th: One Small Thing

Some days do not ask for a new plan or a surge of energy. They ask for one small, real thing.

A glass of water.
A cleared corner of a table.
A slow walk to the mailbox.
A song playing softly in the kitchen while you move through familiar motions.

Small actions have a way of returning you to yourself. They remind you that living is built from simple moments of attention, not dramatic shifts.

You do not have to do everything to be present in your life. You only have to do the next small thing with care.

Today, choose one small action and give it your full attention. Let that be your way of arriving.

January 8th: Winter Details

Winter has a quiet beauty that is easy to miss when you are waiting for it to pass.
Bare branches sketch delicate patterns against the sky. Snow softens edges. The air carries a stillness that feels almost protective.

Nothing in this season asks to impress you. It simply offers what it is.

When you stop expecting more, you begin to notice what has been here all along. The hush. The simplicity. The way the world slows without apology.

Today, notice one winter detail you usually overlook. Let it gently hold your attention for a moment longer than usual.

January 9th: Breathe In Cold Air

Cold air has a way of bringing you back into your body. The first inhale feels sharper. Clearer. You become aware of your lungs, your chest, the simple rhythm of breathing in a way you might not notice indoors.

There is grounding in this. Something honest about feeling the air as it enters you, reminding you that you are here, alive in this moment, connected to the world around you through something as simple as breath.

You do not need insight or clarity to feel present. Sometimes you only need to feel the air in your lungs and the warmth returning as you step back inside.

Today, take three slow breaths in the cold air. Let your body remember how to settle without needing to think your way there.

January 10th: Stay With What's Here

Sometimes the hardest thing to do is nothing at all.

To not reach for distraction.
To not rush toward a version of the future that feels easier to imagine than the present moment.

Another option exists. Staying close.

Staying does not mean liking what is happening. It does not mean approving of discomfort or pretending things are fine. It means allowing the moment to exist without immediately trying to fix it, manage it, or escape it.

Presence is not about calm or relief. It is about honesty. About meeting yourself where you are instead of where you think you should be. About letting what is real have room, even when it feels unfinished or uncomfortable.

Often, staying changes very little on the surface. But inside, something loosens. A breath softens. The body realizes it does not have to flee in order to survive.

Today, choose one moment to remain instead of retreat. Let yourself stay with what's here, trusting that presence alone is enough.

January 11th: The Weight We Carry

There are seasons that quietly reveal what you've been holding. Fatigue settles in. Old emotions rise. Things you pushed aside when life was louder find their way back to the surface.

This is not regression. It is an invitation.

An invitation to acknowledge what has been there all along, waiting for enough space to be felt. You are allowed to notice the weight you've been carrying. You are allowed to admit when something feels heavy, even if you've been strong for a long time.

Naming what you're holding does not make you weaker. It makes you honest. And honesty brings relief in ways denial never can.

You don't have to solve it today. You don't have to release it all at once. Awareness is enough for now.

Today, gently name one thing you've been carrying. Let it be seen without judgment. Let that noticing be a small act of care.

January 12th: Warmth Matters

Warmth is easy to overlook because it feels so ordinary.

The mug in your hands. The blanket pulled a little higher. The quiet relief of stepping into a warm shower at the end of a long day.

These small comforts are not something you have to earn. They are reminders that you are allowed to feel cared for.

You spend so much of your time being capable. Handling what needs to be handled. Moving through your days with effort and responsibility. Warmth asks nothing from you in return. It simply offers itself and waits for you to notice.

There is something deeply human about allowing yourself to be comfortable. About not rushing past the moment where your body softens and your shoulders drop without you trying to make it happen.

Today, linger in one small moment of warmth. Don't hurry through it. Don't treat it as background. Let yourself receive it fully.

January 13th: You're Allowed to Move Slowly

There is a quiet permission written into the natural world. Nothing forces itself to become more than it is ready to be.

Snow falls when it falls. Light returns when it returns. Growth happens beneath the surface long before it ever becomes visible. Nothing apologizes for its timing.

And yet, we often hold ourselves to a different standard. We expect progress on command. Energy on demand. Forward motion regardless of what our bodies or hearts are asking for. We tell ourselves to hurry – to keep up, to push through – even when something inside us is asking to slow down.

Moving slowly is not failure. It is paying attention. It is the practice of listening closely enough to move in rhythm instead of resistance. It is trusting that your pace carries its own wisdom.

You are allowed to take longer than expected. You are allowed to pause. You are allowed to need rest before clarity arrives. You are allowed to move gently without explaining yourself to anyone.

Today, notice where you can release the pressure to hurry. Let your pace be exactly what it is, without asking it to be anything else.

January 14th: A Familiar Sound

There are sounds that quietly define home.
The TV in the background. The hum of the heat. Footsteps in another room. A spoon tapping gently against a bowl.

These sounds rarely ask for your attention, but they are steady proof of a life unfolding around you. They create a backdrop of familiarity that your body recognizes, even when your mind is busy elsewhere.

You are surrounded by small signals of safety and belonging more often than you realize.

Today, pause and listen for one familiar sound in your space. Let it remind you that you are exactly where you are meant to be in this moment.

January 15th: The Day in Front of You

It is easy to feel swallowed by everything that is coming.

All the days ahead. All the things waiting to be handled, decided, figured out. The quiet pressure of what hasn't happened yet.

But you never actually live all of that at once.

You only ever live this day.

This morning light. This set of hours. This small stretch of time that does not ask you to carry anything beyond what is already here.

The day in front of you has its own shape and pace. It does not need you to solve the week, the month, or the season. It asks only that you meet what is in front of you as it arrives.

There is relief in shrinking your focus to what your hands can touch and your eyes can see. In realizing you are not responsible for anything beyond this moment.

Today, stay with the day you are in. Do the next small thing that is yours to do, and stop there.

January 16th: Low Energy Days

Some mornings, your body tells the truth before your mind has time to argue with it.
Heavy limbs. A slower start. A clear awareness that you do not have much to give today.

It can be tempting to resist this. To push harder. To tell yourself you should feel differently. To measure the day against expectations that were never meant for this moment. But some days are not asking for effort. They are asking for gentleness.

Low energy is not a flaw. It is information. An honest signal from your body asking to be listened to rather than overridden. When you ignore it, you drift further from yourself. When you honor it, you stay in relationship with what is real.

Moving slowly is not falling behind. It is a form of responsiveness. A way of meeting the day as it is, instead of forcing it into shape.

Today, let your energy set the tone. Release the need to perform or keep up. Listen to what your body is asking for, and honor it without guilt.

January 17th: What Repeats

There are seasons when repetition becomes impossible to ignore.
The same mug warming your hands each morning. The same place you sit when the day finally loosens its grip. The same path walked again, even after it has been quietly erased and cleared once more.

At first, repetition can feel limiting. Like life has narrowed. Like nothing new is arriving. But over time, something shifts. What once felt monotonous begins to feel dependable. Steady. Almost protective.

There is a kind of grace in what returns each day without asking anything of you. In not having to decide, perform, or reinvent yourself. In allowing certain things to remain constant when so much else feels uncertain or out of reach.

Familiar rhythms do more than fill time. They regulate. They soothe. They remind your body that it is safe enough to rest. That not everything needs attention or change to be worthy.

Repetition, when chosen or received gently, becomes a form of care.

Today, let something familiar hold you. Let it remind you that steadiness is not emptiness, and that being carried can be just as meaningful as moving forward.

January 18th: Ordinary Joy

Joy does not always arrive as excitement.
Sometimes it is a quiet ease that moves through an ordinary moment and disappears if you rush past it.

A comfortable sweatshirt.
A warm drink.
A good stretch.
The way a room looks in late afternoon light.

These moments are easy to overlook because they are not dramatic. But they are often where life feels most real.

Today, notice one ordinary thing that brings a hint of ease. Let yourself linger there and soak it in.

January 19th: Quiet Strength

Strength does not always look the way we expect it to.
It does not always arrive as confidence or certainty. It is not always loud, decisive, or empowering in the way stories often promise. More often, it appears quietly, easy to overlook if you are only watching for something dramatic.

Strength can look like choosing rest instead of pushing.
Like asking for help when silence feels safer.
Like admitting you are tired and continuing anyway – not through force or willpower, but through care and honesty.

This kind of strength does not announce itself. It does not ask to be admired. It is built in moments no one applauds, when you choose gentleness over proving, presence over performance.

It is real.
And it is enough.

Today, honor the quiet strength it takes to keep showing up softly.

January 20th: What Is Already Beautiful

Some days do not need fixing. They need noticing.

The sharpness of cold air as you step outside.
Your breath visible for a moment before disappearing.
Icicles hanging from a roof, catching the light like glass.
The quiet sparkle of frost across a railing or field.

None of this asks anything from you. It simply exists, waiting to be seen.

Beauty does not announce itself loudly. It waits in ordinary places, in small details that are easy to pass by when your mind is busy with plans and lists and thoughts about what comes next.

But when you pause long enough to really look, something shifts. The world feels wider. You feel more present inside it.

Today, let yourself notice what is already beautiful around you, without needing it to mean anything at all.

January 21st: You're Doing Enough

It is easy to believe you should be doing more.

More healing. More growing. More fixing. More becoming. The internal list never seems to end, and the measuring stick always moves farther away.

But there are seasons when doing enough is enough. When showing up honestly matters more than pushing forward aggressively. When presence outweighs progress.

You do not need to justify your pace. You do not need to prove your worth through effort or productivity. You are not behind. You are living at a human pace.

Showing up to your life with honesty, even when it feels messy or incomplete, is already meaningful.

Today, let yourself believe that you are doing enough. Let that belief soften something inside you.

January 22nd: Arriving Without Bracing

There are moments when the space around you grows still. The light softens. The world quiets enough that nothing is immediately required of you.

In these moments, a gentleness becomes available if you don't rush past it. A chance to notice your breath before it tightens or speeds up. The comfort of something familiar close by. The way your body eases when it realizes it doesn't need to be alert or prepared right now.

This is a moment before effort. Before explanation. Before expectation settles in.

Nothing needs to be decided here. Nothing needs to be solved or improved. You don't need to know what comes next or how you'll handle it. You are allowed to simply be where you are, exactly as you are.

So often, we brace ourselves automatically. We anticipate what might be asked. We gather energy before it's needed. But this moment invites something else. It invites you to soften instead of brace.

Today, let this moment unfold at its own pace. Notice how much of you is allowed to rest when nothing is being asked.

January 23rd: When Nothing Is Urgent

Not every moment needs a response.
Not every thought needs action.

There are days that offer space. A pause between obligations. A stretch of time where nothing is pressing, even if your mind insists there should be something demanding your attention.

Stillness can feel uncomfortable if you are used to urgency. Silence can feel unfamiliar if you are used to filling every gap. But there is wisdom in recognizing when nothing needs to be done right now.

You do not need to manufacture purpose in these moments.
You do not need to fill the quiet to make it worthwhile.

Today, notice what happens when you allow stillness to exist. Let the quiet be what it is, without rushing to fill it.

January 24th: Carrying Less

We carry more than we realize. Expectations that were never spoken out loud. Old conversations we replay long after they've ended. Worries that trail behind us through the day like a low hum we've learned to live with.

There are seasons when the pace slows just enough for us to feel the weight of what we've been holding. When distraction fades, what remains becomes clearer. Not because anything new has appeared, but because there is finally space to notice what has been there all along.

You are not required to carry everything forever. Some things were picked up out of habit, not necessity. Some burdens were meant to be held for a time, not for a lifetime.

You are allowed to set something down. Even temporarily. Even just for today.

Today, notice one thing you can carry a little more lightly, and let your body feel the difference.

January 25th: The Way You Speak to Yourself

There is a voice that meets you in quiet moments. It shows up when you are tired, behind, uncertain, or overwhelmed. It comments on your pace. Your choices. Your worth.

This voice has power. It can make a difficult day feel unbearable, or soften it just enough to help you get through. Often, it speaks automatically, shaped by years of expectation, comparison, and pressure.

You do not need to silence this voice or replace it with constant positivity. That is not the work. The work is noticing how you speak to yourself, and choosing not to make things harder than they already are.

You do not need to be endlessly kind. Just a little gentler than yesterday.

Today, practice speaking to yourself the way you would to someone you love. Let your words offer support instead of judgment.

January 26th: Look Around You

Before your mind fills with plans and thoughts, pause and really look around you.

The way light rests on a wall.
The quiet shape of shadows across the floor.
The small details in a room you pass through every day without noticing.

Nothing here is extraordinary. And yet, it is.

The curve of a mug. The grain of a wooden table. The way a plant leans toward a window. The ordinary beauty woven into things you rarely stop to see.

All of it formed with care. All of it part of a world created with intention, down to the smallest details your eyes almost miss.

There is something humbling about realizing you are living inside this. Walking through it. Being held by it without needing to understand how.

Today, let yourself look with fresh eyes and remember that you are surrounded by quiet evidence of thoughtful creation.

January 27th: What You Need Is Enough

It is easy to dismiss your needs. To label them as too much, inconvenient, or unnecessary. To tell yourself others have it harder, so you should keep going without asking for support.

But your needs do not require comparison to be valid. What you need matters because you matter. Full stop.

Care does not have to be earned. It does not need justification. You are allowed to tend to yourself simply because you are here, living inside this body, navigating this life.

Honoring your needs is not selfish. It is honest.

Today, notice one need you have been minimizing. Honor it without explanation or apology.

January 28th: Staying Present

There is a quiet habit of living just ahead of yourself. Thinking about what is next. What still needs attention. What you will deal with once you get through this moment.

But this moment is already here. Your body is here. Your breath is here. The ground beneath you is holding you right now.

Presence does not solve everything. It does not erase discomfort or uncertainty. But it does create steadiness. It gives you a place to stand.

You do not have to arrive fully. You just have to arrive honestly.

Today, gently return to where you are. Let this moment be the only place you need to be.

January 29th: The Pause Between

There are small pauses in every day that you rarely notice.

The moment after you turn off the light.
The stillness after you close a door.
The quiet seconds while you wait for the water to warm.

These pauses are not empty. They are gentle spaces where nothing is required of you. Where you can simply exist without thinking about what comes next.

They are woven into your day more often than you realize.

Today, notice one of these small pauses as it happens. Let yourself enjoy the quiet of it before the next thing begins.

January 30th: What You've Learned Without Trying

Some learning does not come from effort or intention.
It does not arrive through studying, planning, or striving to improve.

It comes from living. From enduring days you did not think you could get through. From paying attention without realizing you were doing it. From noticing what helped you stay, and what quietly drained you.

You have learned things in this season. About your limits. About what sustains you when energy runs low. About what you no longer have the capacity to carry, even if you once did.

This kind of wisdom does not announce itself. It settles into your body. It shows up in the choices you make without thinking. In the boundaries you hold more naturally. In the way you recognize when something is not right for you anymore.

You do not need to summarize what you've learned. You do not need to turn it into insight or meaning.

Trust that it is already part of you.

Today, acknowledge the quiet wisdom you carry, and let it belong to you without explanation.

January 31st: Wired This Way

You may have spent a long time wondering why you feel things the way you do.

Why certain moments stay with you. Why small details affect you deeply. Why the world sometimes feels louder to you than it seems to for others.

But this is not a flaw to solve.

You were made to notice. To feel. To respond to life with depth and awareness.

This sensitivity has carried difficulty at times, but it has also given you empathy, intuition, and a capacity to see what others might miss.

There is nothing wrong with the way you move through the world.

Today, allow yourself to appreciate the way you are wired, without wishing it were different.

February

A season of listening for what is slowly taking shape.

February 1st: The Shift You Notice Later

Some changes happen so quietly you don't recognize them while they're unfolding. Life looks the same on the surface. You move through familiar routines. You tend to what needs tending. Nothing announces itself as different.

And then one day, you notice it.

Something feels less tight than it used to.
A reaction that once took over no longer does.
A pause appears where there used to be urgency.

This is often how growth works. Not through sudden insight or dramatic turning points, but through small internal shifts that settle in gradually. You don't feel transformed. You don't feel finished. You simply feel a little more spacious than you did before.

You don't need to track this.
You don't need to name it or decide what it means.

Simply noticing is enough.

Today, pause long enough to recognize one small shift that may have been unfolding without your awareness. Let it matter, even if it feels subtle.

February 2nd: Held in the Way You Are

Some people move through the world lightly.
Others feel it in their bodies, their breath, their nervous systems.

This isn't something to fix.
It's something to understand.

You may have spent years wondering why things hit you harder, lingered longer, stayed louder. Why what seemed manageable for others felt overwhelming to you.

But depth is not dysfunction.
Sensitivity is not weakness.

You were shaped to notice.
To feel.
To respond.

Today, honor the way you are built. Not everything needs to be overcome. Some things are simply meant to be carried with care.

February 3rd: Still Becoming

You are not behind.
You are not disqualified by the life you've lived.

Nothing about your path was accidental.
What looked like a detour was shaping you quietly, insistently, in ways you couldn't yet see.

You learned in the living.
In the moments that undid you.
In the choices that didn't save you, but taught you.
In the long returns to yourself when there was no shortcut back.

These lessons weren't clean or theoretical.
They were felt. Carried. Lived in your body and breath.
And because of that, they stay with you.

Growth doesn't erase what came before.
It gathers it. Threads it through.
Turning what once felt like damage into discernment, depth, and strength.

You are still becoming.
Not in spite of what you've lived, but because of it.

Today, trust the unfolding that's still happening. Let yourself rise slowly, in your own time.

February 4th: Anchored

Some things arrive quietly and never leave. They don't demand belief or announce themselves in moments of crisis. They simply remain.

Faith can be like that. Not something you reach for when everything falls apart, but something that has been holding you long before you realized you were leaning.

It lives in rhythm – familiar words, repeated gestures, the choice to show up again even when meaning feels thin. And then, one day, what once felt routine becomes essential. What lived at the edges moves to the center.

Faith doesn't fix what hurts. It doesn't erase fear. But it offers steadiness when your hands are shaking and gives you somewhere to stand when everything else feels uncertain.

Sometimes it sounds simple – a whispered plea, a quiet surrender. Not polished. Not impressive. Just honest. And somehow, that is enough.

Faith doesn't ask you to be fearless. It meets you in the trembling.

Today, remember this: you are not carrying this alone. Whatever holds you doesn't require certainty or proof. It only asks that you stay open. You are seen. You are supported. You are held.

February 5th: The Pull Toward What's Next

Even as you remain rooted where you are, part of you may be leaning forward. Imagining change. Wondering what might open. Feeling drawn toward something you cannot yet define.

This pull does not mean you are dissatisfied with the present. It means you are responsive to what is stirring inside you. It means you are listening to a quiet signal of movement, even while your feet stay planted.

Curiosity does not require urgency.
Movement does not require direction.

You are allowed to feel a sense of becoming without needing to name where it leads. You are allowed to hold patience and hope at the same time, without forcing one to cancel the other out.

Today, notice what you feel gently drawn toward. Let it exist without pressure or expectation. Trust that noticing is part of the unfolding.

February 6th: Gentle Persistence

Some days don't ask for inspiration. They ask for persistence.

You wake up and do what needs to be done, not because it feels exciting or meaningful in the moment, but because it matters to you. You tend to what's in front of you. You show up in small ways. You rest when you can.

This kind of effort rarely gets noticed. It doesn't come with recognition or reassurance. And yet, it builds something steady beneath everything else.

Gentle persistence is not about pushing through at all costs. It's about staying connected to yourself while you keep going. It's about honoring your limits while remaining present.

Today, acknowledge one quiet way you showed up – especially if no one else saw it.

February 7th: Making Space for What's Emerging

There are things forming in you that are not ready for definition yet. Ideas. Feelings. Hopes that don't have clear edges.

Nature understands this process. Growth happens long before it becomes visible. What is forming is held quietly, without pressure or demand.

You are allowed the same patience.

You do not need to rush clarity.
You do not need to force answers.
You do not need to name what isn't ready to be named.

Today, leave space for something new to take shape. Let it arrive in its own time.

February 8th: Small Delight

There are small things that make you smile before you even realize it's happening.

A song you didn't expect to hear.
A familiar voice calling your name.
The way sunlight suddenly floods a room.
A memory that surfaces for no reason at all.

These moments don't arrive as lessons. They don't ask for reflection. They simply interrupt the seriousness of the day with something light.

Joy often enters quietly, without announcement. It slips in through ordinary details and leaves just as gently, unless you pause long enough to notice it.

You don't have to go looking for it. It's already woven into your day in ways you usually pass by.

Today, notice one small thing that makes you smile without trying, and let yourself enjoy it fully.

February 9th: Quiet Witness

Some people enter your life and quietly deepen your faith. They do not insist or instruct. They simply live what they believe with steadiness and grace.

Their faith feels breathable. It shows up in how they listen, how they respond to difficulty, and in the calm trust that something larger is holding things together. When they offer a line of scripture or a gentle spiritual truth, it does not feel imposed. It arrives like fresh air, right when you are ready.

They seem to sense when words are needed and when silence is enough. Their belief is not something they use to persuade, but something they carry with humility and care.

Being near this kind of faith reminds you that belief does not have to be loud to be strong. Sometimes, witnessing someone else's devotion is enough to help you remember your own.

Today, notice the people whose quiet faith has strengthened you. Let yourself receive what they offer without pressure or explanation, trusting that inspiration often arrives exactly when it is needed.

February 10th: The Space Between Tasks

There are small pauses woven into your day that often go unnoticed. The few seconds before the coffee is poured. The brief pause while you wait for a traffic light to change. That moment after you finish one task and before you reach for the next. The breath you take without thinking about it.

These spaces are easy to rush past. But when you pause inside them – even briefly – something softens. The body settles. The mind loosens its grip. You remember you are more than the list you're moving through.

You don't need to create more time.
You don't need to slow everything down.
You only need to notice the time that already exists between things.

Today, linger in one small pause. Let it be a place to land, even for a moment.

February 11th: What You Carry Forward

Not everything you've lived through needs to follow you into what comes next. Some experiences were meant to teach you, shape you, and then be set down.

This can be difficult to recognize. We grow attached to our stories – even the painful ones – because they once helped us make sense of who we were. But discernment asks a different question: what still supports you, and what has quietly become too heavy?

Letting go does not erase the past. It doesn't deny what you survived or learned. It simply acknowledges that you are allowed to move forward without carrying every weight with you.

Today, notice one thing you may no longer need to carry. Let yourself imagine how it might feel to travel lighter.

February 12th: The Courage to Be Unfinished

There is a quiet pressure to be resolved. To have answers. To know where you're headed and why. To feel certain enough to relax.

But much of life is lived unfinished. In process. In motion without clear direction or tidy conclusions.

There is courage in allowing yourself to be here – incomplete, evolving, still learning – without withholding care from yourself until you feel more put together. You do not need to be fully formed to be worthy of gentleness.

Being unfinished is not a flaw. It is a state of becoming.

Today, allow yourself to be unfinished without needing to move ahead of where you are.

February 13th: Softening the Grip

Notice where you're holding tightly.
In your jaw. In your shoulders. In the way your thoughts keep circling plans and contingencies, rehearsing what might go wrong before it has a chance to go right.

This grip doesn't come from control. It comes from care. From wanting to protect what matters. From loving deeply and trying to stay one step ahead so nothing gets lost, nothing falls apart, no one gets hurt. You learned to hold things this way because at some point, it felt necessary.

But holding too tightly asks your body to stay braced. It keeps your breath shallow. It turns vigilance into habit. And over time, what began as care can quietly become strain.

Softening your grip doesn't mean letting go of responsibility or turning away from what matters. It means trusting that you don't have to manage every outcome to be safe. That life can meet you without being forced into shape. That you are allowed to exhale without something slipping through your fingers.

Often, relief doesn't arrive through effort or fixing. It arrives when you allow yourself to loosen. When you stop gripping long enough to feel the ground beneath you again.

Today, choose one place to soften – one expectation, one plan, one moment where you let your shoulders drop. Notice how your body responds when you release, even just a little.

February 14th: The Ways We Stay Connected

Connection does not always look like closeness in the obvious sense. Sometimes it lives in thought – carrying someone with you as you move through the day. Sometimes it shows up as affection offered freely, without agenda. Sometimes it's the simple awareness that love exists, even when you are not actively reaching for it.

There are connections that feel steady and grounding, shaped by time and shared life. And there are connections that feel light, bright, and uncomplicated – the kind that remind you of joy, innocence, and the ease of being loved just for who you are.

In quieter seasons, connection becomes more intentional. You notice the warmth in small gestures. A shared smile. A remembered laugh. A gentle check-in that says, I see you. I'm here. I care.

Love does not belong to one shape or one story. It moves through relationships of all kinds – within family, romantic, chosen, and unexpected. It shows up in presence, attention, and the simple act of holding someone in your heart.

Today, notice one way you feel connected. Let it be tender. Let it be joyful. Let it matter more than you usually allow.

February 15th: When It No Longer Holds

There comes a moment when you realize that something you once relied on no longer supports you in the same way. What used to help now feels heavy. What once offered relief now asks for more than you can give.

This awareness doesn't arrive with drama. It comes quietly. Through fatigue. Through the sense that continuing as you are requires more effort than you are willing to give.

You may feel grief for what once carried you. You may feel uncertainty about what comes next. That does not mean you failed. It means you are listening more honestly than before.

Some things serve us for a season. They help us survive. They get us through. And then, without becoming wrong, they stop being the right support.

Today, notice what no longer feels sustaining. You don't have to fix it or release it yet. Simply allowing yourself to see it clearly is already a meaningful shift.

February 16th: Living With Absence

Some losses do not announce themselves loudly. They move in quietly and rearrange the shape of everyday life. An empty space where something used to be. A habit you reach for before remembering it's gone.

Grief often lives here – not in dramatic moments, but in ordinary ones. In the pauses. In the subtle awareness that life is different now, and there is no going back to the way it was.

You may not have words for this. You may not feel strong or steady. That is okay.

And even here, you may find yourself held in ways you can't fully explain. There were seasons when faith wasn't something practiced. It was something that carried you when you had no strength left.

Today, allow one gentle moment of remembrance. Let absence be acknowledged with care.

February 17th: When You Stop Numbing

There is a particular bravery in staying present with discomfort. In feeling what you once learned to avoid. In letting emotions rise without immediately reaching for something to quiet them.

At first, this can feel overwhelming. Without old distractions or escapes, everything seems louder. Sharper. More demanding of your attention.

But presence builds strength slowly. Not by fixing pain, but by teaching you that you can survive it. That you can feel deeply and still remain.

You are not alone in this, even when it feels that way.

Today, notice one feeling without needing it to change.

February 18th: The Strength of Showing Up

Some people love in quiet, consistent ways. Not with speeches or grand gestures, but through reliability. Through being there again and again. Through doing what needs to be done without needing recognition.

This kind of presence is easy to overlook because it doesn't ask for attention. It's built into the everyday – meals made, rides given, work finished, care offered without keeping score. A steadiness that becomes part of the foundation of your life.

There is strength in this simplicity. In choosing responsibility. In staying when things are ordinary, imperfect, or inconvenient. In offering support not because it's dramatic, but because it matters.

Showing up does not require perfection. It requires commitment. A willingness to stay engaged, to carry your share, to be counted on. Over time, this kind of love shapes people. It teaches safety. It teaches trust. It teaches what dependability feels like in the body.

Today, notice one way someone has shown up for you quietly and consistently. Or one way you do this for others. Let yourself recognize the power of steady presence – and how much it means to be able to rely on someone who stays.

February 19th: Learning to Stay

There are moments when the urge to leave is strong.
Not always physically. Often internally. You scroll, distract, busy yourself, or reach for something that dulls the edge of what you're feeling.

Staying asks something different.
It asks you to remain present long enough to notice what's actually happening inside you. To feel discomfort without immediately fixing it, numbing it, or turning it into a story you can manage.

This doesn't mean forcing yourself to endure what harms you. It means choosing honesty over avoidance. Letting the moment exist as it is, without rushing past it just to feel better.

Staying builds trust slowly. Not because the feeling disappears, but because you learn that you can be with yourself through it. That you don't vanish when things are hard. That you are still held, even here.

Today, practice staying with one moment a little longer than usual. Let yourself discover that presence can be steadier than escape.

February 20th: Choosing Differently

Change rarely happens in grand gestures or dramatic decisions. More often, it unfolds quietly, in choices so small they almost go unnoticed.

One pause instead of reacting.
One different response.
One moment where you choose care over habit.

These choices may not feel significant at the time. No one applauds them. No one sees the internal shift that just occurred. But they matter. They shape the direction of your life in ways that only become clear later.

You are not asked to be perfect. You are not required to overhaul everything at once. You are simply invited to notice when a different choice is possible.

Sometimes grace moves through willingness, not certainty.

Today, notice one small choice you can make that supports who you are becoming, and let that be enough.

February 21st: Trusting Your Capacity

There comes a moment when you begin to realize you are stronger than you once believed. Not because life became easier, but because you stayed. You learned. You adapted in ways you never planned to.

This strength is not loud. It does not announce itself as confidence or certainty. It shows up quietly, in how you move through hard days with more awareness. In how you respond with care instead of panic. In how you no longer collapse in places that once overwhelmed you.

You did not become this way by accident. You were shaped by what you lived through, and by what carried you when you could not carry yourself.

You have already survived more than you give yourself credit for.

Today, acknowledge one way you trust yourself more than you once did. Let that recognition settle into your body.

February 22nd: The Weight You No Longer Carry

There are days when you suddenly notice something feels lighter. Not because life has changed dramatically, but because you are no longer holding something the way you once did.

It might be a habit.
A role you felt obligated to play.
A story you kept repeating about who you had to be.

You did not set it down all at once. There was no clear moment of release. You loosened your grip slowly, often without realizing it, until one day you noticed the absence of strain.

This kind of release rarely comes with ceremony. It arrives quietly, in the relief you feel when you stop trying so hard to maintain what no longer fits.

Today, notice one thing that feels lighter than it used to. Let yourself honor that shift, even if you cannot fully explain how it happened.

February 23rd: The Space Boundaries Create

When you stop overextending yourself, space appears. At first, it can feel unfamiliar. Even a little uncomfortable. You may wonder what to do with it, or whether you are allowed to have it at all.

But this space is not emptiness.
It is room to breathe.
Room to listen.
Room to remember who you are when you are not constantly responding to everyone else's needs.

Boundaries do not push life away. They create the conditions for life to meet you more honestly. They protect what is essential so it can remain intact.

Learning to rest inside this space can take time. It asks you to trust that you do not have to fill every gap to be worthy.

Today, notice where a small boundary has created space. Let yourself rest there without rushing to fill it.

February 24th: Learning to Trust the Quiet

Not every moment of quiet needs to be filled.
Not every pause means something is missing.

Sometimes quiet is simply the nervous system settling after long seasons of vigilance. The mind catching its breath. The body realizing it is safe enough to soften.

If you have spent years moving quickly, staying busy, or holding everything together, quiet can feel unsettling at first. It may even feel lonely. But with time, it becomes a place you can return to. A place that does not demand performance or explanation.

Quiet does not mean nothing is happening. Often, it is where the deepest work takes place.

Today, sit with a moment of quiet and notice how your body responds. Let yourself trust that stillness can hold you.

February 25th: When You Choose Yourself Gently

Choosing yourself does not always look bold or decisive. Most of the time, it happens quietly, in moments no one else witnesses.

It looks like saying no without offering a long explanation. Like resting before exhaustion forces you to stop. Like noticing resentment beginning to form and choosing care instead of pushing past it. These choices do not announce themselves as breakthroughs. They feel small. Almost ordinary.

And yet, they matter deeply.

Each time you choose yourself gently, you reinforce a truth that may not have always felt safe to believe. That your needs deserve attention. That your body and heart are worth listening to. That you do not have to abandon yourself to be accepted or loved.

You do not need to justify these moments. You do not need permission. You do not need to make them visible for them to count.

Today, notice one quiet way you choose yourself. Let it be yours, without needing it to be anything more.

February 26th: Carrying Compassion Forward

It can be tempting to look back on past versions of yourself with harshness. To replay moments and wish you had known better. To imagine different choices, different outcomes, different endings.

But compassion changes how memory lives in the body.

When you meet your past with compassion instead of judgment, something softens. The tight grip of shame loosens. The nervous system exhales. You begin to see not failure, but effort. Not weakness, but survival.

You learned what you could, when you could, with the tools and awareness you had at the time. Nothing more was available to you then.

Carrying compassion forward does not mean excusing harm or pretending things were easy. It means honoring the reality of what you lived through and the strength it took to keep going.

Today, offer compassion to a past version of yourself. Let it rest there without needing to rewrite the story.

February 27th: Trusting the Small Signs

Hope does not always arrive as certainty or confidence. Often, it comes quietly, slipping in through moments that are easy to overlook.

It might be a feeling that lingers a little longer than doubt. A decision that feels more aligned than the ones before it. A moment of calm where there used to be tension or fear. Nothing dramatic. Nothing conclusive. Just enough to notice if you are paying attention.

These small signs are easy to dismiss because they do not shout. But they matter. They are evidence of movement, even when the season still looks the same on the surface.

Change does not always announce itself with clarity. Sometimes it asks only for awareness.

You do not need proof. You do not need guarantees. You only need presence.

Today, notice one small sign that something is shifting, and let yourself trust it.

February 28th: Look Up

Before you move into what's next, pause and look up.

At the sky. At the light shifting across it. At the quiet movement of clouds you normally don't notice because your eyes are fixed on what's in front of you.

The world is larger than the thoughts you've been carrying. Larger than the questions you've been turning over. Larger than the work you've been doing inside yourself.

Sometimes relief comes not from figuring anything out, but from remembering you are standing inside something vast, steady, and already in motion.

Nothing asks you to solve it. Nothing asks you to understand it. It simply exists around you, holding more than you can see.

Today, look up for a moment and let yourself feel small in a way that brings peace, not pressure.

March

The first soft signals that something is beginning to shift.

March 1st: The First Hint of Change

Some mornings feel different before you can explain why. The air shifts just enough to notice. The light feels closer, less distant than it did before. You still reach for your coat. You still move carefully. And yet, something underneath it all has begun to ease.

Change rarely arrives with certainty. It does not always come with clarity or confidence or a clear sense of direction. More often, it arrives as a quiet awareness you can't quite name. A subtle feeling that you are no longer standing in the exact same place you were, even if nothing on the outside has changed yet.

This kind of change does not ask for decisions. It does not require you to act or commit or move faster than you're ready to. It simply asks to be noticed. To be respected for what it is – a signal, not a command.

Sometimes the most important shifts begin as whispers. As gentle reminders that life is still moving, even when it has been quiet for a long time.

Today, notice the first hint of change without asking it to become anything more. Let awareness be all that's needed for now.

March 2nd: What Catches Your Eye

There are moments in a day that pull your attention without asking permission.

A color. A sound. A face. A movement outside a window. Something that makes you look twice without knowing why.

You don't have to understand it. You don't have to make meaning from it. You only have to notice that something in you is curious.

Curiosity is a quiet sign that you are present. It doesn't ask for effort. It simply draws you toward what is already here.

Today, notice what catches your eye for no reason at all, and allow yourself to follow that small thread of interest.

March 3rd: The Truth That Surfaces

When things begin to soften, truth has more room to surface. Not the loud, confrontational kind. But the quiet realizations that rise when there is finally enough space to hear them.

You may begin to see something more clearly than you could before. What you want. What you no longer have the capacity to tolerate. What you have been outgrowing without fully admitting it to yourself. These truths often arrive gently, but they can still feel tender.

Clarity does not always feel relieving at first. Sometimes it feels destabilizing. Sometimes it simply feels honest in a way you are not used to holding yet.

Truth does not demand immediate action. It does not require you to make changes before you are ready. Often, it asks only for acknowledgment. For permission to exist without being argued away.

Today, gently name one truth that feels ready to be seen. Let it rest with you, without needing to decide what comes next.

March 4th: Moving Without Forcing

There can be movement without urgency.
Forward motion without pressure.

Forcing yourself ahead often comes from fear – fear of falling behind, fear of missing something, fear that if you don't push, nothing will happen at all. But there is another way to move. One that listens instead of demands. One that follows responsiveness rather than pressure.

Moving without forcing means staying connected to yourself as you take a step. It means noticing when something feels supportive instead of draining. It means trusting that progress does not require constant effort to be real.

You are allowed to move at a pace you can sustain.
You are allowed to take steps that feel steady rather than impressive.

Today, choose one action that feels aligned instead of rushed. Let that be how movement happens.

March 5th: Being Seen Gently

There are times when staying quiet feels natural. When keeping to yourself feels steady and safe. When you move through the day without needing much attention from anyone.

And then, slowly, something shifts.

You notice yourself speaking a little more freely. Sharing a thought without rehearsing it first. Letting your presence be felt without trying to minimize it.

Being seen doesn't have to be dramatic. It doesn't require you to explain yourself or reveal everything at once. Sometimes it looks like a small moment of honesty. A relaxed posture. A willingness to take up the space you're already in.

You may not even realize you're doing it. You simply stop shrinking in places where you no longer need to.

Today, notice one small way you allow yourself to be visible, without effort or performance.

March 6th: What Feels Easier Than Before

You may not notice it at first.

Something you once avoided no longer feels quite as heavy. A situation that used to tighten your chest now passes with less resistance. A task you once postponed feels more neutral than it did before.

This doesn't mean everything is different. It doesn't mean you've arrived somewhere new. It simply means that your relationship to certain things has shifted quietly over time.

There is a gentle kind of relief in this. Not dramatic. Not triumphant. Just a sense that you are moving through parts of life with a little more steadiness than you once had.

You don't need to analyze why. You don't need to turn it into proof of growth. You can simply notice it.

Today, pay attention to one thing that feels slightly easier than it used to, and simply notice it.

March 7th: Letting Experience Change You

What you live through leaves a mark.
Not always in obvious ways, but in how you respond, what you tolerate, and what you no longer ignore.

There is wisdom in allowing yourself to be shaped by experience instead of trying to return to who you were before it happened. Growth is not about erasing what came before. It's about integrating it. Carrying forward what strengthened you and releasing what no longer needs to come with you.

Some lessons were hard-earned and deserve respect. Others have done their work and can be set down without guilt.

Change does not betray who you were.
It builds upon it.

Today, notice one quiet way you've been changed by what you've lived. Let that change be honored, even if it still feels unfinished.

March 8th: When Things Begin to Soften

When thawing begins, it is rarely graceful.
Snow melts into mud. Ice loosens unevenly. What was once held in place starts to move, and not all of it looks pretty or organized.

Inner seasons behave the same way. As things soften, emotions surface. Memories rise. Feelings you tucked away during colder months come back asking to be felt. What you managed to hold together through stillness may feel less contained now.

This mess is not a setback. It is not a sign that something is wrong. It is evidence that movement has begun.

You are not required to make sense of everything immediately. You are not asked to clean it all up or turn it into clarity. Some parts of thawing simply need room.

Today, allow what is surfacing to exist without judgment. Let the mess be part of the process, not a problem to solve.

March 9th: When You Notice Your Strength

There are moments when you surprise yourself.
Not with something dramatic or visible, but with how you respond.

A pause where there once was reaction.
A breath where there used to be panic.
A choice that feels steadier, kinder, more grounded than it once did.

This strength did not appear overnight. It was built gradually. Through days when you kept going even when things felt uncomfortable. Through moments when you chose presence over escape. Through times when you stayed with yourself instead of abandoning what you felt.

You may not always recognize this strength while it's forming. It does not announce itself. It reveals itself slowly, in hindsight, when you realize you handled something differently than you once would have.

Today, notice one small way your response feels calmer or more rooted than it used to. Let yourself acknowledge how far you've come.

March 10th: When Grief Changes Shape

Grief does not disappear.
It shifts. It softens. It moves through your life in different forms as time goes on.

Some days it feels close, pressing against you in ways that take your breath away. Other days it sits quietly in the background, woven into ordinary moments. A song that catches you off guard. A scent that opens a memory. A place you did not expect to miss so much.

Grief is not a sign that you are stuck. It is a sign that love continues to live inside you, even as life changes around it.

There may have been seasons when grief carried you because you had no strength left to carry yourself. And there may be seasons now where it walks beside you more gently.

Today, acknowledge one place where grief still visits. Meet it with tenderness instead of resistance. Let it be part of your life without letting it define all of it.

March 11th: What Isn't Yours to Hold

Some people grow used to noticing what others need before it's spoken. Adjusting. Anticipating. Making room without thinking about it.

Over time, this can become so natural that you no longer see it happening. You simply carry what's around you because you always have.

And then, occasionally, you notice the weight of it.

Not as blame. Not as regret. Just as a quiet awareness that you've been holding more than you realized.

There is something gentle in recognizing this. A small shift in how you stand inside your own space. A soft understanding that not everything around you requires your hands.

Today, notice one place where you allow something to remain outside of you, without reaching to pick it up.

March 12th: Staying

There are moments when leaving would be easier.

Not physically. Internally.

Reaching for distraction. For noise. For anything that blurs the edges of what you're feeling.

And then, sometimes, you don't.

You stay.

You sit in the moment long enough to feel what is actually there without trying to soften it, fix it, or escape it.

This kind of staying is quiet. No one sees it. No one applauds it. But it changes something steady inside you.

Today, notice one moment where you remain with yourself just a little longer than you used to.

March 13th: Choosing Honesty Over Approval

There is a quiet shift that happens when you stop measuring yourself by how comfortable others feel around you. When you begin to value honesty more than approval.

This does not happen all at once. It begins in small moments. A pause before agreeing. A truth spoken gently instead of swallowed. A choice to let someone feel disappointed rather than abandoning yourself.

Choosing honesty does not mean becoming harsh or uncaring. It means allowing yourself to be real, even when it feels awkward. Even when it disrupts old patterns. Even when you are not sure how it will be received.

Approval can feel safe, but it often comes at a cost. Honesty, while riskier, creates room to breathe.

Freedom often begins here.

Today, notice one moment where you choose honesty over pleasing. Let yourself feel the steadiness that follows.

March 14th: Trusting Who You Are Becoming

You are not who you were a season ago.
Not because you changed everything, but because you stayed awake to your life.

You paid attention. You noticed what hurt, what healed, what drained you. What quietly sustained you. You learned what you can no longer ignore, and that knowing lives in your body now. Steady. Earned. Not just an idea.

Becoming does not always feel like forward motion. Sometimes it feels like uncertainty. Like standing in a place where the old ways no longer fit and the new ones are still forming.

You do not need to rush ahead. You do not need to prove anything.
You are already on your way.

Today, pause and trust the person you are becoming. Even if the path is still unfolding. Especially then.

March 15th: What You No Longer Reach For

There was a time when certain things felt necessary.
Automatic. Familiar. Like the only way through a difficult moment.

You may notice now that you don't reach for them the same way.
Not because you decided to stop.
Not because you forced yourself to change.
But because something inside you no longer asks for them.

This can be easy to miss.
The absence of an old reflex.
The quiet space where an old pattern used to live.

Nothing dramatic has to happen for this to be real.
Sometimes growth is simply what you no longer feel pulled toward.

Today, notice something you don't reach for the way you once did, and let yourself recognize how far you've come without needing to explain it.

March 16th: Letting Feelings Move

Feelings are meant to move.
To rise. To crest. To pass through.

Many of us learned to interrupt them. To push them down. To rush past them before they could fully be felt. Staying composed often felt safer than staying honest.

Sometimes emotions arrive without warning. Old grief. Unexpected tenderness. A wave of feeling that does not fit neatly into words.

This can feel unfamiliar. Even overwhelming. Especially if you've spent a long time holding yourself together.

You do not need to control what you feel. You do not need to understand it right away. Giving it a little room is often enough.

Feelings tend to move more easily when they are not resisted.

Today, notice one feeling as it passes through, and allow it a little space.

March 17th: The Choice to Stay Grounded

Life has a way of filling up.
Requests. Expectations. Noise. Movement.

Staying grounded becomes a choice – not something you achieve once, but something you return to. You choose it in how you breathe when things feel rushed. In the way you speak to yourself when pressure rises. In noticing when your body is signaling that enough is enough.

Grounding does not mean withdrawing or slowing everything down. It means staying connected to yourself while life moves. Letting your feet remain planted even when the world feels loud.

You don't need to do this perfectly.
You only need to notice when you've drifted and return.

Today, choose one simple way to come back to yourself. Let it be steady, not elaborate.

March 18th: When Old Patterns Appear

Old patterns do not disappear just because you have outgrown them.
They tend to resurface when you are tired, overwhelmed, or unsure. When your nervous system is stretched. When something feels unfamiliar or tender.

You may catch yourself reacting in ways you thought you had moved past. Thinking thoughts you believed were behind you. Reaching for habits that once helped you cope but no longer fit the life you are building.

This does not mean you are going backward. It means you are human. Growth does not erase the past. It changes how you meet it.

What matters is not whether the pattern appears, but how quickly you notice it and how gently you respond. Awareness is not failure. It is progress in real time.

Today, notice an old pattern without judgment. Let recognition be enough. Let compassion meet you where you are.

March 19th: Choosing Care Over Control

Control can look a lot like responsibility.
Planning ahead. Staying vigilant. Trying to anticipate every outcome so nothing falls apart.

But control tightens the body. It narrows the breath. It keeps you braced, always preparing for what might go wrong.

Care feels different. Care listens instead of demands. It responds instead of forcing. It makes room for uncertainty without abandoning yourself in the process.

You may notice moments when the urge to grip tighter shows up. To manage instead of tend. To stay in your head instead of your body.

Today, notice where control feels like tension. See if you can soften just enough to choose care instead, even if nothing around you changes.

March 20th: Trusting the Pace of Change

Change does not move in a straight line.
It advances, pauses, circles back, and sometimes seems to undo itself before finding its way again.

There may be days when trust feels natural and days when doubt returns without warning. This does not erase your growth. It is part of it. Progress does not require constant confidence to be real.

Trust grows when you stop measuring every moment. When you stop asking whether you're doing it right and start allowing the process to unfold.

Your pace does not need comparison.
Your path does not need explanation.

Today, trust the rhythm of your change. Let it move as it needs to, without interference.

March 21st: Standing in the Middle

There is a place between who you were and who you are becoming.
A place where old habits no longer feel right, but new ways have not fully taken shape yet.

Standing here can feel uncomfortable. Unsteady. You may feel impatient to arrive somewhere clearer. You may wonder if you are stuck, or doing something wrong, or taking too long.

But this middle space is not failure. It is transformation in motion. It is where integration happens. Where old identities loosen and new ones are quietly forming beneath the surface.

Nothing is required of you here except presence.

Today, honor yourself for standing in the middle. Let yourself exist without rushing to resolve what is still unfolding.

March 22nd: When You Breathe a Little Deeper

There are moments when you catch yourself breathing more fully without trying.
Your shoulders drop. Your jaw unclenches. Your breath moves lower, slower, more naturally.

These moments often arrive quietly. While washing dishes. While walking from one room to another. While standing in the light without thinking about it. You may not even realize how much you were holding until the holding releases.

This is your body learning something new. Learning that it is safer now than it once was. Learning that it does not need to stay braced all the time.

These small softenings matter. They are signs of trust rebuilding from the inside out.

Today, notice one moment when your body softens. Let it stay a little longer than usual. Let yourself believe that ease is allowed.

March 23rd: The Space You're Creating

As you begin to make different choices, space opens around you almost without asking permission.
Time you once filled automatically.
Energy you once spent managing, explaining, proving, or holding things together.

At first, this space can feel unsettling. You might feel the urge to rush in and fill it. To stay busy. To replace what you've set down with something familiar, even if it no longer fits. Emptiness can feel risky when you're used to constant motion.

But this space is not emptiness.
It is room.
It is possibility.
It is where your life gets to meet you more honestly, without performance or pressure.

Not all space needs to be used right away. Some space is meant to be lived in gently before it's filled with anything new.

Today, notice one place where space has opened around you. Resist the urge to rush into it. Let it hold you for a moment longer than feels comfortable.

March 24th: When You Listen to Yourself

There is a voice inside you that speaks quietly.
It does not shout.
It does not demand attention.
It simply offers guidance when you slow down enough to hear it.

For a long time, you may have learned to override this voice. To prioritize what others expected. To choose what felt safer, more acceptable, or less disruptive. Listening to yourself now can feel unfamiliar, even risky. You may wonder if you can trust what you hear.

But this voice has not disappeared. It has been waiting patiently, growing steadier with each moment you turn toward it.

Listening does not mean acting immediately. It means acknowledging what is true for you without dismissing it.

Today, listen for your own inner guidance. Let it speak without interruption. Honor what it says, even if all you do is notice it.

March 25th: The Practice of Self-Respect

Self-respect is rarely built through grand declarations.
It grows through small, consistent actions.

Keeping a promise to yourself when no one else would know.
Saying no without overexplaining or apologizing.
Leaving when you are tired instead of pushing yourself past your limit.

These choices can feel uncomfortable at first. You may worry how they will be received. You may feel the old pull to justify yourself or smooth things over. But each time you choose self-respect, you reinforce something important.

You teach your body and heart that your needs matter.
That your limits are worth honoring.
That you can be trusted to care for yourself.

Respect grows quietly through repetition, not perfection.

Today, practice one small act of self-respect. Let it count, even if no one else sees it.

March 26th: Allowing Joy Without Guilt

Moments of joy can arrive unexpectedly.
A laugh that surprises you.
A sense of ease in your body.
A moment where you feel present without trying.

Joy can feel complicated when you have known pain. You might hesitate, wondering if it's allowed. You might brace yourself, expecting it to fade. You might feel a quiet guilt for enjoying something while parts of your life still feel tender.

But joy does not ask for permission.
It does not erase what you have lived through.
It does not minimize grief or struggle.

Joy and sorrow can exist together. One does not cancel the other.

Today, if a moment of joy appears, see if you can receive it without questioning it. Let it move through you freely, without needing to explain why it belongs.

March 27th: What You No Longer Argue With

There comes a moment when you stop trying to convince yourself that something is fine when it is not.
You stop negotiating with your own knowing.
You stop explaining away the discomfort that keeps returning.

This shift does not always come with clarity or certainty. Often, it arrives as relief. A quiet exhale. A sense of no longer forcing yourself into places, roles, or patterns that no longer fit.

You may not have all the answers yet. You may not know what comes next. But you know what you can no longer argue with.

Listening to this knowing is not dramatic. It is honest. It is an act of trust in yourself.

Today, notice one truth you no longer need to debate. Let yourself stand in it gently, without rushing to resolve anything else.

March 28th: Standing on New Ground

You may not feel entirely steady yet, but you are standing on different ground than you were before.
The footing is unfamiliar. The terrain has shifted. What once felt certain may no longer be there in the same way. And still, you are upright. Present. Here.

This ground is not polished or predictable. It has been shaped by what you've lived through, by the moments you stayed when leaving felt easier, by the choices you made quietly when no one was watching. You are learning how to support yourself in new ways now. How to pause instead of react. How to choose instead of default. How to stay present with your life as it unfolds rather than rushing ahead of it.

This is not the end of the journey. It is a beginning shaped by care rather than urgency. A beginning that trusts you to listen before you move.

Today, acknowledge the new ground beneath you. Feel your feet there. Let yourself stand with intention, even if steadiness comes slowly.

March 29th: When You Trust Yourself a Little More

There are moments when you notice something subtle but significant. You no longer second-guess every choice. You pause. You listen inward. You decide without immediately scanning for reassurance or approval outside yourself.

This trust did not arrive all at once. It grew quietly through trial and error. Through moments when you listened and felt the difference. Through moments when you didn't, and learned what that cost you. It grew through staying present long enough to discover that you can handle what follows your choices, even when the outcome isn't perfect.

Self-trust is not loud or dramatic. It doesn't announce itself as confidence. It simply shows up when you need it, steady enough to lean on.

Today, notice one decision you make from trust rather than fear. Let that awareness settle into your body. Let it remind you that you are learning how to be your own safe place.

March 30th: Letting the Past Rest

The past has a way of resurfacing when you least expect it.
A memory stirred by a smell.
A feeling that arrives without warning.
A version of yourself you thought you had already outgrown.

You don't need to push these moments away. You don't need to dissect them or turn them into lessons. Sometimes the most respectful thing you can do is acknowledge what appears, thank it for what it once taught you, and let it rest again.

Not everything that returns is asking to come with you. Some things simply want to be seen one last time before they settle back into place.

You are not meant to carry everything forward. You are allowed to travel lighter now.

Today, allow one memory or feeling from the past to pass through without gripping it. Let it move on without needing to follow it.

March 31st: Divinely Timed

There are people you stumble upon in this life who arrive without warning or plan, yet feel anything but accidental. You cross paths in ordinary ways. A conversation you almost didn't have. A place you nearly didn't go. And still, something in you recognizes them. A quiet pull. A sense that this meeting matters before you know why.

These connections often meet you in tender seasons. When you are searching, healing, or standing on the edge of change. Through shared moments, honest words, or simply their steady presence, they leave an imprint. Something shifts. Something softens.

Looking back, it becomes hard to believe it was chance. It can feel as though God placed them gently in your path, knowing exactly what your heart needed at that moment. They may stay for a season or a lifetime, but their presence is never wasted.

Today, notice one person whose arrival in your life felt guided rather than planned. Let yourself trust that what touched you deeply was not random.

April

Learning how to move forward without rushing what's unfolding.

April 1st: When the World Reappears

There is a particular kind of noticing that happens in early spring. Not excitement exactly, but awareness. A sense that the world is present again in a way it hasn't been for months. Not loud or demanding, just quietly asking to be seen.

You might catch it in small, almost ordinary moments. The sound of birds outside a window you kept closed all winter. The way sunlight stretches across the floor a little farther each afternoon, lingering where it once disappeared too quickly. The instinct to open a window before remembering the air is still cool, still waking up.

After a long season of turning inward, this outward pull can feel unfamiliar. You may feel relief alongside vulnerability, as if life is inviting you back into participation before you feel fully ready. There can be tenderness in this noticing, a sense of exposure after so much quiet.

You do not have to meet this moment with enthusiasm or certainty. You do not need to rush toward it or make sense of it yet. Curiosity is enough. Allowing yourself to notice without obligation is enough.

Today, notice one way the world feels more present around you. Let yourself meet it gently, without asking anything more of the moment than it is offering.

April 2nd: The Love That Feeds Others

There is a kind of love that expresses itself through preparation. Through hands busy in the kitchen. Through tables set a little more fully than necessary. Through the quiet instinct to make sure everyone is taken care of before sitting down yourself.

This love shows up consistently, woven into the rhythm of family life. Because it is so reliable, it can be easy to overlook. It's often expected, rarely announced, and quietly taken for granted – even as it holds everything together.

This love does not rush. It plans. It anticipates. It notices who needs a little extra and offers it without being asked. It understands that nourishment is not only about food, but about presence, comfort, and belonging. You feel it in the small details – an extra chair pulled up, food saved for later, the way someone senses what you need before you say it.

There is generosity here that doesn't seek recognition. A steady giving that becomes memory, tradition, and safety all at once. The kind that shapes a family without ever needing credit.

Today, notice the love that feeds others in your life – the kind that shows up so faithfully it can be easy to miss. Let yourself pause long enough to appreciate it.

April 3rd: Beginning Without Certainty

Some beginnings arrive before clarity does.
A step taken without knowing how it will unfold.
A yes spoken before the whole picture is visible.
Movement that allows for pausing, adjusting, changing course along the way.

There is no script here. No guarantee.
Only a quiet willingness to try while questions linger unanswered.

Often, this is how meaningful things begin.
Not from confidence or control, but from curiosity and courage.
From showing up before readiness is confirmed.
From noticing that understanding tends to arrive through movement, not before it.

Certainty does not lead the way.
The ending remains unseen.
And still, the first step is taken.

Today, notice where a small beginning might be asking for permission rather than assurance.

April 4th: Listening for What You Want

During winter, desire often grows quiet.
Survival takes precedence. Energy turns inward. Life narrows to what feels manageable, practical, safe.

As things begin to open again, something may stir.
Longings that were set aside. Wants left unnamed. Questions about what you miss, what you hope for next, what draws your attention now that there is room to notice. The feeling can be both tender and unsettling.

Wanting something brings vulnerability with it.
It hints at possibility. It reveals care. It opens you to being changed. After a season of protecting yourself, even acknowledging desire can feel like a risk.

There is no urgency here.
No need to act, justify, or make it sensible. Sometimes naming a desire quietly is enough.

Today, listen for one small want. Let it exist without judgment. Let it be gently known.

April 5th: Responding Differently

Growth is rarely dramatic.
It doesn't always announce itself with bold moments or visible milestones. More often, it shows up quietly, in the way you respond.

A pause where there once was reaction.
A familiar pattern noticed, then softened.
A limit recognized and honored.
A kinder voice in moments that once carried pressure or self-criticism.

These moments can seem small. Easy to overlook.
And yet, they suggest something shifting beneath the surface.
Awareness beginning to take root where habit once led.

Not every change feels like progress. Some of it feels ordinary. Unremarkable.
But ordinary is often where transformation lives.

Today, notice one small way your response has changed. Let it count.

April 6th: Following the Body's Signals

Sometimes the body notices a shift before the mind finds language for it.
An urge to move a little more. A stretch that happens without planning. The pull to step outside, even briefly. Fatigue lifting in small ways – not gone, but lighter than before.

For a long time, those signals may have been overridden. Pushed through. Managed.
Now, listening begins to feel different. Less like effort. More like trust.

There is no need to force renewal. No requirement to be disciplined or productive.
Only a quiet curiosity. A responsiveness to what feels supportive rather than demanding.

Growth does not need to be driven.
It can unfold one signal at a time.

Today, follow one cue from your body with care instead of force. Let it guide you gently.

April 7th: Opening Without Overgiving

This season carries a sense of opening.
Ideas begin to stir. Conversations feel possible again. There may be a readiness to connect, to participate, to say yes where no once felt necessary.

And still, openness has its own edges.
It does not ask for endless availability. It does not require giving beyond what feels sustainable. Receptivity can exist without overextension. What is new can be welcomed without abandoning what keeps you well.

There is a learning here.
A quiet distinction between expansion that nourishes and expansion that drains.

You can move toward life and remain intact.

Today, notice where openness and self-respect meet. Let them exist side by side.

April 8th: The Unevenness of Growth

Growth rarely looks the way we imagine it will. Some days you feel open, capable, steady. Other days, old heaviness returns without warning, and you wonder where your progress went.

This can be unsettling. You may question yourself. Doubt what you felt before. Wonder if the shift was imagined. But growth is not constant expansion. It includes movement, retreat, and return.

Spring itself doesn't arrive all at once.
It hesitates. Cold mornings interrupt warm afternoons. A bud closes again after opening, then opens once more. Growth happens anyway.

Your inner seasons follow the same rhythm.

Today, let your growth be uneven without questioning its validity. Trust that something is still unfolding, even when it doesn't look linear.

April 9th: When the Past Feels Closer

Some days carry an echo.
A memory surfaces unexpectedly. A feeling arrives that belongs to another time, another version of you.

This isn't a return to where you started.
It's the present brushing against something unfinished. Often, what matters reappears only when there is enough safety, enough space, enough steadiness to hold it.

There is no need to analyze the moment or turn it into insight. No need to fix what shows up. Sometimes noticing is enough. Caring is enough.

The past doesn't surface to pull you backward.
It surfaces to be met differently.

Today, meet one memory with gentleness rather than resistance. Let your response be softer than it once was.

April 10th: Carried

There are seasons when effort stops working. When willpower thins. When the practices that once held you feel just out of reach.

When you can't generate strength from inside yourself, you begin to notice what has been holding you all along. In those moments, faith isn't something you perform. It's something you allow.

It shows up quietly – not as answers, but as steadiness. As the sense that you don't have to understand everything to keep going, or be strong in order to be supported.

Faith meets you where you are, not where you think you should be. It doesn't ask for eloquent words or perfect trust. Sometimes it begins with nothing more than a breath and a simple asking.

Being carried doesn't mean you stop walking. It means you stop pretending you're doing it alone.

Today, loosen your grip just enough to feel what's already holding you. Let that be sufficient.

April 11th: Trusting What Feels Different Now

You may begin to notice subtle shifts. Situations that once felt overwhelming no longer carry the same weight. Your reactions soften. Your recovery comes faster. What once sent you spiraling now simply registers and passes.

This doesn't mean life has become easier. It means you are meeting it differently. With more space. More awareness. More steadiness than you had before.

These changes are easy to dismiss because they're quiet. But they are earned. Built through attention, patience, and choosing presence again and again.

Trust what feels different now. Let yourself acknowledge it without minimizing or questioning it.

Today, name one way something feels different than it used to – and let that matter.

April 12th: Letting Joy Arrive Carefully

Joy often arrives quietly. It shows up in small moments – a laugh that surprises you, a sense of ease that wasn't there before, a flicker of lightness that feels almost unfamiliar. And just as quickly, you may find yourself bracing, waiting for it to disappear.

If you have known loss or disappointment, this hesitation makes sense. Your nervous system learned to protect you by staying alert. Joy can feel risky when you've been taught that good moments don't last.

But joy does not ask to be defended. It does not require you to hold your breath or prepare for disappointment. It simply asks to be noticed while it is here.

You don't have to trust joy completely yet. You don't have to believe it will stay. You only need to let it exist without interruption.

Today, allow yourself to enjoy one small moment without preparing for its end. Let joy arrive and pass on its own terms.

April 13th: Staying Honest With Yourself

There can be a quiet pull to perform wellness. To appear healed. Confident. Put together. As if growth means having answers or presenting a finished version of yourself.

But honesty matters more than appearances. You are allowed to still be figuring things out. You are allowed to feel steady one day and unsure the next. Growth does not require polish.

Being honest with yourself creates a steadiness no performance ever could. It allows you to stay grounded instead of split – one version of you on the outside, another quietly carrying what's unresolved.

You don't need to explain yourself. You don't need to impress anyone, including yourself.

Today, check in with yourself honestly. Name what is true without judgment or pressure to fix it. Let honesty be what holds.

April 14th: Letting the Day Be What It Is

Some days don't unfold the way you pictured.
Plans bend. Skies change. Rain arrives where sun was expected.

There was a time when this would have felt like a disruption. Something to push against. A reason to tighten or rush or feel disappointed. But now, there is another option. To slow. To notice. To let the day take its own shape instead of forcing it into the one you planned.

Rain doesn't ruin the day.
It changes the texture of it. The sound. The pace. The way you move through your hours. Footsteps soften. Conversations slow. The world asks less of you.

Not everything unexpected is an obstacle. Some things arrive to invite a different rhythm. A gentler way of moving. A small release from how you thought the day should go.

Today, allow the day to be what it is. If something shifts, see if you can stay open long enough to discover what it offers.

April 15th: When You Notice Your Voice

There may be moments now when you hear yourself speak and notice something different. Fewer explanations. Less apologizing. More clarity about what you mean and what you don't.

This shift didn't come from practicing the right words. It came from listening to yourself long enough to trust what needed to be said. From realizing you don't need to earn space by over-justifying your presence or softening your truth.

Your voice hasn't become louder. It has become steadier. More rooted. Less reactive.

You are speaking from alignment instead of habit.

Today, notice one moment where you speak from truth rather than reflex. Let yourself feel how different that steadiness is.

April 16th: The Choice to Respond Slowly

When life starts to pick up speed, messages arrive sooner, decisions ask for answers, and the pace around you quickens.

You may notice a moment between receiving and responding. A breath. A hesitation that isn't avoidance, just space. A chance to feel what's true before anything is said.

Not every response needs to be immediate.
Some clarity comes after the body settles. After the urgency passes. After you listen inward instead of keeping up.

Waiting can feel unfamiliar at first. Old worries may surface. And still, the pause offers something else: steadiness, care, and a response that doesn't require rushing past yourself.

Today, notice one place where you allow yourself to respond more slowly. Let the space support what comes next.

April 17th: Noticing What Returns

As energy rises, familiar impulses may drift back into view. Not loudly. Not urgently. Just a subtle remembering of what once felt automatic.

You notice it now.
Without surprise. Without panic. Simply as something that passed through before and has passed through again.

Awareness changes the texture of the moment.
There is more space than there used to be. More choice. Even when nothing is decided yet.

This isn't a step backward.
It's a sign that you're present enough to notice what's moving inside you.

Today, meet one familiar urge with steadiness. Let noticing be enough.

April 18th: Learning to Receive

Many people learn how to give early on. How to offer support. How to show up. How to anticipate needs before they are spoken. Giving becomes familiar, even comfortable. It creates a sense of purpose and belonging.

Receiving can feel much harder. It asks you to soften your guard. To pause instead of reaching. To trust that what is being offered does not come with a cost you need to repay. Receiving asks you to believe that you are worthy of care without effort or explanation.

This can feel vulnerable, especially if you learned that love had to be earned or that independence was safer than reliance. Letting something come toward you can stir discomfort, even when it is kind.

Spring models a different way. The earth receives light and rain without apology. It does not rush to prove its worth. It opens and allows what nourishes it to arrive.

Today, allow yourself to receive one small kindness without deflecting it. Let it land. Let it stay. Notice what softens when you don't push it away.

April 19th: When You Set a Boundary and Stay

Setting a boundary is one thing. Staying with the feelings that follow is another.

After you say no or name a limit, you may feel a familiar wave of guilt or doubt. You may replay the moment, wondering if you were too much or not enough. You may feel the urge to explain yourself further, to smooth things over, to undo what you just did.

This response is common for anyone who learned to keep the peace at their own expense. Your nervous system remembers that approval once felt like safety.

But staying with a boundary does something important. It teaches your body that safety does not depend on pleasing everyone. It builds trust between you and yourself. It shows you that discomfort can be survived without retreating.

Today, notice how it feels to stay with a boundary instead of backing away from it. Let the discomfort rise and fall. Trust that it does not mean you were wrong.

April 20th: Trusting Your Inner Timing

There is a rhythm inside you that doesn't respond well to rushing.
It notices when things are pushed forward too quickly, and when they're held back out of fear. It reacts quietly, through tension or restlessness, through ease or resistance.

The world moves on schedules and expectations. Deadlines. Comparisons. Noise.
But something deeper moves differently. It waits for readiness. For a sense of alignment that can't be forced.

You may have felt this before.
The discomfort of acting too soon. The dull ache of waiting too long. Somewhere between those two is a pace that feels alive and steady at the same time.

Nothing has been missed.
What is meant to take shape does not arrive through urgency.

Today, listen for the pace that feels natural to you. Let that rhythm guide what comes next.

April 21st: Standing More Firmly

There is a subtle shift that happens when you stop questioning your right to take up space. When you no longer brace yourself before speaking. When you realize you don't need to shrink, soften, or justify yourself in order to belong.

You stand differently now.
Not rigid. Not defensive. Just settled. There is less effort in how you hold yourself. Less negotiation in your posture and presence.

This steadiness didn't come from forcing confidence.
It grew slowly, through moments of choosing yourself. Through boundaries you held. Through truth you spoke even when your voice shook.

You are not performing strength.
You are living it.

Today, notice one way your body holds this shift. Let it be felt, not analyzed.

April 22nd: When Something Feels Different

There is a moment when you notice something has shifted. Not dramatically, and not all at once. Just enough to register in your body before your mind catches up.
You breathe a little deeper without trying. Your shoulders ease. The space around you feels less tight than it did before.

Your body often recognizes change before your thoughts do. Something loosens. Something inside you responds quietly, without needing explanation or certainty.

This is how openness begins. Not through effort or intention, but through sensation. Through the subtle awareness that it may be safe to soften just a little.

You don't need to respond perfectly.
You don't need to do anything with this noticing.
Simply recognizing the shift is enough.

Today, pay attention to one small way your body responds differently than it used to. Let that awareness be gentle and unforced.

April 23rd: What You Let In

The world carries more input than it did before.
More voices. More information. More requests for your attention.
You may feel yourself becoming more alert, more aware of what's happening beyond your immediate inner world.

This can be energizing and overwhelming at the same time.
You are not required to take everything in.
Discernment matters now. You get to choose what nourishes you and what becomes background noise.

Living outward again does not mean losing yourself.
It means learning how to stay connected to what matters while allowing the rest to pass by without gripping it.

Today, notice one thing you allow to reach you. Let the rest soften into the background.

April 24th: Letting Color In

Color returns slowly. Not all at once, and not in the places you expect first. The faintest green at the edge of the yard. A brighter jacket pulled from the back of the closet without much thought. Something blooming quietly before you realize you've been looking at it for days.

Color has a way of lifting the spirit without explanation. It bypasses logic and effort. It reminds you that life has been moving beneath the surface even when everything felt muted or still. Even when you weren't sure anything was happening at all.

You don't have to search for joy or force optimism. Sometimes renewal arrives through the senses first – through sight, through beauty, through a small moment that catches your attention and softens you without asking permission.

Today, notice one color that draws your eye. Let it brighten the moment without needing it to mean anything more.

April 25th: When Movement Feels Inviting

Sometimes it begins without a decision.
A longer walk than you planned.
A stretch that takes a little more time.
The choice to stay outside a few minutes longer, without needing a reason.

Nothing about it feels urgent.
Nothing is being corrected or improved. The body responds, and you follow.

There is a rhythm here that doesn't ask for discipline or intention.
Just attention. Just presence.

Today, notice one moment when movement happens naturally. Let it unfold without directing it.

April 26th: The Courage to Soften

There are times when rigidity loosens.
Expectations relax. Defenses ease.
Places where you once held yourself tightly begin to soften without effort.

This softness can feel unfamiliar.
You may notice yourself more affected by things you once brushed past. More open. More tender.
Softness is often misunderstood as weakness, but it is what allows responsiveness, connection, and growth.

Without softness, nothing new takes root.
Without it, life becomes something to manage rather than meet.

Today, notice one place where you feel softer than you used to. Let that softness be a strength, not something you rush to protect yourself from.

April 27th: Staying With the Mess

Spring is not tidy. Melting snow reveals debris that's been hidden for months. Gardens look unfinished long before they look beautiful. Growth begins in disorder, not polish.

You may notice this reflected in your own life now. Unfinished conversations. Feelings that don't resolve neatly. Parts of yourself that feel in-between – no longer who you were, not yet who you're becoming.

This mess is not a mistake. It is not evidence that you're doing something wrong. It is part of the process. Becoming is rarely clean, and clarity often comes only after you've stayed with what feels unresolved.

Today, stay with something unfinished without rushing it toward closure. Let it be incomplete and still worthy of your care.

April 28th: Trusting the Season You're In

There's a temptation to want growth to hurry up. To want visible proof that things are moving fast enough. To look around and wonder if you should be further along by now.

But seasons unfold at their own pace. Buds open when they're ready. Roots deepen long before anything shows. Much of what matters happens underground, unseen and unmeasured.

You are allowed to trust this timing – in the world around you and within yourself. You don't need to force the next stage or apologize for where you are. This moment has its own purpose.

Today, name the season you feel yourself in. Let it be exactly that, without comparison or pressure to advance.

April 29th: Noticing Who You're Becoming

Sometimes growth shows itself not in big changes, but in how naturally you move through your life. In the way you speak with more confidence. In how you hold yourself. In the ease that begins to replace effort.

You may not have noticed the shift as it was happening. Growth like this doesn't rush or announce itself. It unfolds quietly, through experience, through trial and tenderness, through showing up again and again. One day, you simply realize you are standing differently in your own life.

There is something beautiful about witnessing that kind of becoming – in yourself or in someone you love. The way strength and softness learn to coexist. The way kindness deepens without losing its light. The way authenticity starts to feel less risky and more natural.

This kind of growth doesn't ask for praise or proof. It speaks for itself. It lives in presence, in self-trust, in the quiet confidence of knowing who you are and who you're still allowed to become.

Today, take a moment to notice who you are becoming. Let yourself feel proud – not because you're finished, but because you're growing with care.

April 30th: Standing at the Edge of What's Next

The end of a month carries a particular kind of awareness. Not a finish line, and not quite a beginning. More like a ledge you can stand on long enough to feel where you are before moving again. A place to breathe and look back without judgment, and forward without pressure.

The season is no longer theoretical. It's happening. The ground beneath you has softened. Light lasts longer. There is evidence of growth all around you, even if it isn't complete or polished. And the same is true within you. You are no longer just imagining change or preparing for it. You are living inside it. Responding in real time. Learning through experience rather than intention alone.

You may feel both steadier and more uncertain than you expected. That's not a contradiction. It's what happens when you're actually moving. When you're no longer standing at the doorway of your life, but inside it, adjusting as you go.

There is no need to hurry forward. No requirement to define what comes next before you're ready. You are allowed to pause here. To feel your weight in your body. To notice what has shifted since you last stood at this edge. To recognize what you've learned simply by staying present.

Today, stand at the edge of what's next without rushing across it. Let yourself arrive fully where you are. Trust that when the next step becomes clear, you will know how to take it.

May

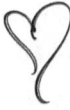

Growth that comes from staying present, not pushing ahead.

May 1st: When the Day Feels Larger

Some mornings feel wider than others.

You wake up and the day does not feel heavy or distant. It feels open. The light is brighter. The air moves differently through the room. Even before you have words for it, you sense that something in you is more awake than it was before.

Not dramatic. Not loud. Just present.

You may notice it in simple ways. Opening a window without thinking. Lingering a moment longer before moving. Feeling curious about the day instead of bracing for it. Life doesn't feel like something to get through. It feels like something you are inside of.

There were seasons when getting through the day was the work. When energy was carefully measured and attention turned inward just to stay steady. Those seasons mattered. They shaped you. But this is a different kind of day.

This is a day that meets you with a little more space. A little more breath. A little more room to engage without force.

You don't need to do anything special with it. You don't need to make it meaningful. You only need to notice that you are here, and the day feels larger around you than it once did.

Today, step into the day without rushing it. Let yourself feel the openness before filling it.

May 2nd: Choosing Each Other

Long-term love isn't built in grand gestures.

It's built in the life you share quietly. In the spot on the couch that's always yours, next to theirs. In the way dinner appears – a familiar meal, made without needing to be asked. In the steady care of a home – snow shoveled, leaves raked, the small, practical acts that say *I've got this* before you even notice.

This kind of love isn't about staying because you have to. It's about choosing the life you've grown into together. Learning how to move at each other's pace. Slowing down when one of you needs it. Reaching back without keeping score. Trusting that neither of you has to rush ahead alone.

Love like this doesn't announce itself. It shows up in laughter at the end of long days. In shared glances across the room. In the instinctive way their hands ease the tension in your neck when you sit near them – no conversation, just care. A quiet knowing that you are held.

This is love that understands timing. That knows when to lead and when to wait. When to stand steady and when to soften. Not perfect, not polished – but deeply faithful to the life you're walking together.

Today, honor the love that chooses presence. The kind that stays close, adjusts, and keeps walking – side by side – again and again.

May 3rd: The Vulnerability of Being Seen

With more light comes more visibility. You may find yourself more present in the world now, stepping into spaces where your voice, your presence, or your choices are more noticeable than they've been in a while.

And being seen, even in good ways, can stir old discomfort. The urge to perform. To over-explain. To soften yourself so no one can misunderstand you. To become easier to receive before you let yourself fully arrive. These instincts usually come from a desire for safety, not vanity. Many of us learned early that being fully ourselves could carry consequences.

So you learned to edit. To adjust. To manage the room before the room managed you.

But being seen does not require perfection. It does not ask you to become someone else. It asks only for honesty. For showing up as you are, without excessive adjustment or self-erasure. It asks you to trust that you can tolerate someone else's response without letting it rewrite who you are.

You do not need to shrink to belong. You do not need to polish yourself to be worthy of presence.

Today, allow yourself to be seen in one small, genuine way. Speak one honest sentence without dressing it up. Wear what feels like you. Let yourself take up the space your life already occupies. Let it be imperfect. Let it be real.

May 4th: When Wanting Feels Safe Again

Desire returns differently after hard seasons. At first, it can feel cautious, almost shy. A quiet curiosity rather than a bold declaration, like something peeking out from behind a door it once kept locked for survival.

And then one day, you notice it clearly. You want connection. You want experiences. You want more than survival or maintenance. You want to be touched by life again, not just get through it.

This wanting is not reckless or greedy. It is not a failure of contentment. It is a sign that something inside you feels safe enough to reach again. For those who have lived through disappointment, grief, addiction, anxiety, burnout, or long seasons of bracing, desire can feel like a risk. Wanting means hoping. Hoping means opening. Opening means feeling.

So when wanting returns, it's tender. It's brave.

Desire does not demand immediate action. It doesn't need to be chased or justified. It can simply inform you, like a small light turning on inside your chest, gently pointing toward what matters now.

Today, sit with one desire without rushing to fulfill it. Don't turn it into a task. Just listen. Let it reveal what you care about in this season, and let that be enough.

May 5th: Moving Without Disappearing

There are moments when momentum quietly takes over.
A quick yes. A faster reply. A sense of moving ahead before you've fully arrived.

You might notice it in the body first. A tightening. A restlessness. The feeling that your attention has jumped ahead of you, leaving something behind. It's familiar. Times when staying in motion felt easier than staying present.

And sometimes, there is a pause.
Not always. Not perfectly. Just a small moment of awareness before you move on. Enough to notice what you feel. Enough to choose how you continue.

Movement doesn't have to pull you away from yourself.
It can include pauses. Check-ins. A willingness to move at a pace that keeps you connected to what's happening inside you.

Today, notice one moment where you stay with yourself while moving forward. Let that be enough.

May 6th: Trusting What Holds You

There are times when life begins to widen and you realize how little control you actually have. Plans multiply. Possibilities appear. The future feels less contained. And with that openness can come a quiet fear – the sense that if you don't manage everything carefully, something will slip through your hands.

Faith offers a different way of living inside that uncertainty. Not by giving you answers, but by reminding you that you are not responsible for holding everything together on your own. That there is something steady beneath the movement, something that does not depend on your effort or vigilance.

Trust does not mean passivity. It means releasing the belief that every outcome rests on your shoulders. It means showing up faithfully, doing what is yours to do, and allowing the rest to unfold without force.

You are not being asked to figure it all out. You are being asked to stay open. To remain willing. To believe that you are supported even when the path ahead isn't fully visible.

Today, practice letting one thing rest in hands other than your own. Offer it up. Release it. Trust that what holds you is strong enough to meet you here.

May 7th: The Practice of Showing Up

There is something steady and beautiful about giving your attention to something you care about.

It might be a sport, a hobby, a subject, or a quiet interest that slowly grows. Whatever it is, when you show up for it again and again, you begin to learn more than the thing itself. You learn patience. You learn commitment. You learn how to try, adjust, and keep going.

You learn how to give effort without needing an audience.

Over time, this kind of steady attention shapes you. It teaches you how to stay with what matters. How to work hard without losing heart. How to care deeply while still leaving space to notice the world around you.

And sometimes, alongside the doing, a softer way of seeing appears. A pause. A moment of noticing. A reminder that life is not only meant to be pursued, but also observed.

The way you give yourself to what you love is quietly shaping who you are becoming.

Today, notice what you return to with care, and allow yourself to be fully there.

May 8th: When Old Patterns Try to Return

As life fills in again, familiar patterns may resurface quietly. Not as crises or obvious setbacks, but as habits that once felt automatic. The reflex to say yes before checking in. The urge to smooth things over. The instinct to stay busy instead of staying present with what you feel.

You may notice it mid-sentence or halfway through a decision. That moment when awareness catches up and you realize you're about to step into something that once felt normal but no longer feels right in your body. There is often a brief pause there, a choice point that didn't exist before.

And that pause is everything.

This noticing matters. It means you are awake now in a way you weren't before. You are no longer moving purely on instinct or conditioning. You are present enough to see yourself in real time. Present enough to choose.

Old patterns returning does not mean you are failing. It means you are practicing awareness in a fuller life. It means you're meeting the real test: not how you behave in a quiet season, but how you stay aligned when life gets loud again.

Today, pause when an old pattern appears. Don't attack it. Don't label it as "bad." Meet it with curiosity instead of judgment. Ask, What am I trying to protect right now? Let the pause itself be the progress.

May 9th: The Emotional Weight of Expansion

Growth carries weight too. As your life expands, you may feel more responsibility, more visibility, more emotional exposure. There is more to hold, more to tend, more to feel.

This can be surprising. You may have expected growth to feel light or liberating, only to find that it feels tender instead. Heavier in a different way. Not oppressive, but requiring more presence and care. Like carrying something precious: not because it's too much, but because it matters.

You are not failing at expansion. You are learning how to hold more without abandoning yourself. Learning how to stay grounded while your life becomes fuller. Learning how to remain connected instead of overwhelmed.

There is a difference between weight that crushes and weight that strengthens. One drains you. The other teaches you how to carry yourself differently. One asks you to numb. The other asks you to show up.

Today, acknowledge one place where growth feels heavy. Offer yourself compassion instead of critique. Let care meet you where responsibility has increased.

May 10th: Letting the Body Catch Up

There can be a difference between where your thoughts are and where your body is.
The mind moves ahead. The body lingers.

You might notice it as fatigue that arrives without warning. A heaviness in the shoulders. A tightening in the stomach during moments that feel otherwise fine. Rest asking for more time. Energy arriving in waves instead of all at once.

Nothing is necessarily wrong.
The body has its own timing. It remembers differently. It responds through sensation long before it offers explanation.

Some days, listening looks like pausing.
Other days, it looks like choosing less. Or saying yes more slowly. Or letting rest count without turning it into something to justify.

Today, notice one request your body makes. Let it guide the pace, even briefly.

May 11th: The Quiet Work of Trust

Trust does not arrive fully formed. It builds quietly, through repetition. Through moments when you show up, make a choice, and see that you can handle what follows.

You may notice yourself trusting your instincts more often. Or questioning them with less harshness. Or simply pausing long enough to hear what you actually feel before responding. You stop outsourcing every decision. You stop needing ten signs from the universe and three people's approval before you honor what you already know.

This kind of trust doesn't announce itself as confidence. It feels steadier than that. Less dramatic. More rooted. It grows when you stay with your decisions instead of abandoning yourself at the first sign of discomfort. When you don't punish yourself for being human. When you let experience teach you instead of shame.

Trust that is rushed becomes brittle. Trust that is practiced becomes resilient.

Today, honor one small moment where you trusted yourself and stayed with that choice. Let that quiet success matter.

May 12th: When You No Longer Need to Prove

There is a particular relief in realizing you no longer need to prove your worth through effort or endurance. That you do not have to earn rest. That your needs do not require justification.

This realization often arrives quietly. Through exhaustion that clarifies what you're done performing. Through moments of honesty where you choose not to explain yourself one more time. Through the decision to stop over-functioning. Through noticing how often you've been trying to be "good" at life, instead of present for it.

You begin to understand that proving was never the same as belonging. That effort was never the same as worth. That being needed is not the same as being loved.

You are allowed to exist without performance. Without justification. Without constantly demonstrating your value.

Today, notice one place where you stop trying to prove yourself. See what happens when effort softens, even for a moment.

May 13th: Allowing Joy Without Bracing

There are moments when joy appears unexpectedly.
A laugh that feels unforced. A moment of ease that surprises you. A sense of contentment that arrives without warning.

And almost immediately, the body remembers.
The instinct to brace. To wait for the other shoe to drop. To remind yourself not to settle in too fully. This reflex has a history. It formed when joy and loss lived close together. When good moments didn't always stay.

Bracing keeps sweetness at a distance.
It turns joy into something you skim rather than inhabit. Something you hold lightly, nervously, instead of letting it settle.

Joy doesn't ask to be defended.
It doesn't need preparation or protection. Only presence.

Today, if joy shows up, notice the urge to brace – and see what happens if you don't. Stay with the moment a breath longer. Let it be felt while it's here.

May 14th: Standing in Your Life

There are moments when you realize you are no longer standing on the sidelines of your own life. You are here now. Participating. Making choices that reflect who you are becoming, not who you were trying to be.

This does not mean you feel fearless or completely certain. It means you are present. Willing to stay. Willing to engage without waiting for perfect conditions. You're no longer delaying your life until you feel like a better version of yourself. You're bringing your real self to the day you actually have.

Often, we learn how to do this by watching others. By being close to people who show us what it looks like to pay attention, to show up fully, to inhabit their lives with care. Their presence becomes an invitation, reminding us that life doesn't ask for perfection, only participation.

Presence is a powerful form of commitment. It says, I am here with what is, instead of I'll arrive once everything feels safer. You are no longer postponing your life until you feel ready. You are living it as readiness unfolds.

Today, notice one way you stand more fully in your life. If someone has helped show you how to do this, let yourself feel the quiet gratitude of having learned by example.

May 15th: When Clarity Replaces Urgency

There was a time when urgency felt like motivation. When moving quickly felt safer than waiting. Decisions were made on momentum rather than clarity, simply to avoid missing out or falling behind.

Now, something else is happening. You pause more often. You listen longer. You notice how your body responds before you commit. You can feel the difference between excitement and pressure. You can tell when something is truly yours, and when it's just loud.

This isn't hesitation. It's knowing. It's the understanding that not every opportunity is yours to take, and not every open door requires an immediate yes. It's recognizing that your peace belongs in the decision.

This way of choosing protects your energy. It honors your values. It allows your life to unfold with intention instead of impulse.

Today, notice one place where you choose clarity over urgency. Trust that choice. It reflects a quieter, steadier kind of wisdom taking root.

May 16th: Letting Things Be Easier

Ease can feel unfamiliar if you've spent a long time bracing. When things begin to soften, you might question it. You might wonder if you're missing something, if you're being careless, if you're letting your guard down too much. Old instincts can whisper that ease is earned only after exhaustion.

But ease does not mean avoidance. It does not mean a lack of care or commitment. It means you are no longer carrying weight that was never meant to be yours. It means you've learned the difference between effort that matters and effort that drains you without giving anything back.

There was a time when doing everything the hard way felt necessary. Survival often demands that. But survival is not the same as living. And you are allowed to live differently now.

Ease is not something you force. It's something you allow once you trust that you no longer need constant vigilance to stay safe.

Today, allow one thing to unfold with less effort. Maybe you don't over-explain. Maybe you accept help. Notice what happens when you stop bracing and let yourself be supported by what's already in motion.

May 17th: When You Don't Override Yourself

There are moments when your body speaks clearly. A tightening in your chest. A racing heart. Sweaty palms. A quiet but unmistakable no that rises before you have words for it.

In the past, you may have learned to override these signals. To talk yourself out of them. To push through discomfort in the name of being helpful, agreeable, or strong. You may have learned that keeping the peace mattered more than listening inward. That your value came from your ability to endure.

But not overriding yourself is an act of respect. It tells your body that its signals are trustworthy. It tells your nervous system that safety does not depend on self-abandonment – that what you often call anxiety is not a malfunction, but a system that learned to protect you.

Listening does not always mean dramatic change. Sometimes it looks like a quiet pause. A slower response. A choice not to explain yourself.

Today, honor one signal from your body or intuition without justifying it or talking yourself out of it. Let yourself recognize this as your body's way of protecting you.

May 18th: The Freedom of Not Fixing

You don't need to solve everything. Not every feeling needs a plan. Not every discomfort needs immediate relief. There is a particular exhaustion that comes from believing it's your job to make everything better all the time.

Fixing often comes from fear. Fear that if you don't act quickly, things will fall apart. Fear that sitting with uncertainty means something is wrong. Fear that you'll be blamed if someone is uncomfortable. So you rush in, you smooth, you manage, you carry, and you call it love, even when it's costing you.

But presence asks for something else entirely.

Presence allows things to exist without rushing them toward resolution. It trusts that clarity can emerge through patience, through staying, through allowing emotions and situations to unfold without being controlled.

There is freedom here. Freedom in realizing that not every moment is a problem to solve. Some moments simply ask to be lived.

Today, resist the urge to fix one thing. Stay with it instead. Breathe. Let it be unfinished. Notice what softens when you stop trying to manage the outcome.

May 19th: Choosing What You Protect

As your life fills with more connection and possibility, protection becomes intentional. Not in the form of walls, but in the form of care. Not withdrawal, but thoughtful choice.

You begin to see more clearly what drains you and what sustains you. Which spaces ask too much. Which relationships require constant explanation. Which commitments leave you depleted instead of supported. And you realize that your peace is not something you sacrifice as proof of your goodness.

Protecting your energy is not selfish. It is how you ensure that what matters most remains intact. It is how you honor your limits and respect the life you are living.

Protection does not mean shutting down. It means choosing carefully where you place your attention and effort. It means you stop offering your best self to what leaves you empty.

Today, choose one thing to protect – your time, your rest, your peace, or your focus. Let that choice be an act of care, not guilt.

May 20th: Living With Fewer Apologies

You may notice that you apologize less now. Not because you've stopped caring, but because you've become clearer. Clearer about your limits. Clearer about what is yours to carry and what is not.

You stop apologizing for needing space. For saying no. For choosing rest. For being honest about what you can and cannot give. You begin to recognize the difference between accountability and unnecessary self-erasure. You learn that an apology is sacred when it's real, and exhausting when it's just habit.

This shift is subtle, but it's so powerful. It changes how you take up space. How you speak. How you move through the world without constantly shrinking yourself to make others comfortable.

You are not becoming harder. You are becoming more grounded.

Today, notice one place where you let go of an unnecessary apology. Let your presence speak for itself.

May 21st: Trusting the Life You're Building

You may not be able to see the full shape of your life yet. The edges are still forming. The details are unfinished. But you can feel its direction. You can sense it in the choices you're making, in the way your decisions align more closely with who you are now rather than who you once needed to be.

This trust does not come from certainty. It comes from repetition. From showing up again and again with honesty, even when clarity is incomplete. From choosing care over control. From noticing that when you listen inward, things tend to settle instead of unravel.

You are building something real. Something rooted. Even if it is still taking form, even if parts of it feel fragile or undefined, it is yours. And it is growing in the direction of truth.

Today, pause and trust the life you're building. Place a hand on your heart and the other on your belly, and remind yourself: I'm not lost. I'm becoming. Let yourself believe that what is unfolding makes sense, even if you can't see the whole picture yet.

May 22nd: When Joy Feels Less Fragile

In the beginning, joy can feel like something you have to hold carefully. As if it's temporary. As if relaxing into it might make it disappear. You enjoy it, but you keep one eye on the exit, waiting for the moment it slips away.

Over time, something shifts. Joy stops feeling borrowed and starts feeling earned. Not because life has become perfect or predictable, but because you trust yourself more fully inside it. You know you can handle what comes next. You know you can survive the ebb as well as the flow. You know that if joy leaves for a while, you will not disappear with it.

Joy becomes something sturdier. Something you can stand in without bracing. Something that doesn't require you to hold your breath.

Today, notice one moment of joy and let yourself stay with it a little longer. Let your shoulders soften. Let your breath deepen. Let your body learn that joy does not always have to be fleeting to be safe.

May 23rd: The Comfort of Being Yourself

There is a quiet relief that comes when you realize you no longer need to manage how you are received. You show up with fewer rehearsals. Less editing. Less effort spent anticipating how others might react.

This doesn't mean every interaction feels easy or comfortable. It means you are less willing to abandon yourself to make things smoother. You stop performing likability. You stop softening truths that need to be spoken. You let yourself be real, even if it's imperfect.

Comfort grows when you stop pretending. When you trust that being yourself is not a risk you need to mitigate, but a place you are allowed to stand.

Today, notice one moment where being yourself feels easier than it used to. Let that ease remind you how far you've come.

May 24th: When the Body Feels Like Home

As the days warm, you may notice a subtle shift in how you inhabit your body. Movement feels less forced. Rest feels more nourishing. There is less resistance and more cooperation between you and the physical space you live in every day.

This relationship did not heal overnight. It changed through patience. Through listening. Through choosing care again and again, even when frustration or distrust tried to take over. It changed because you stayed. You returned. You made peace in small ways before it ever became a big, triumphant thing.

Feeling at home in your body is a form of belonging you carry everywhere. It's a quiet refuge. A place you can return to no matter where you are.

Today, offer your body one moment of appreciation or care. Stretch like you mean it. Step outside and let sunlight touch your skin. Drink water slowly. Place a hand on your chest and say, thank you. Let your body know you see the work it has done to carry you here.

May 25th: Letting the Present Be Enough

There is a strong pull to look ahead. To plan the next step. To measure progress. To ask whether you're doing enough, becoming enough, arriving fast enough.

But there are moments when the present feels complete on its own. Nothing needs to be added. Nothing needs to be improved. The moment simply is, and that is sufficient.

Letting this be enough does not mean you stop growing or dreaming. It means you stop rushing past your life in order to reach some imagined future. It means you allow yourself to arrive where you already are. It means you stop treating your current life like a waiting room.

Today, notice one moment that feels complete just as it is. Maybe it's coffee in quiet. Maybe it's the way the light hits the floor. Maybe it's a normal, unremarkable minute where nothing needs to be fixed. Let yourself rest there without reaching for what comes next.

May 26th: Trusting What Comes Naturally

When you stop forcing yourself into roles, rhythms, and expectations that don't fit, something unexpected begins to happen. Life starts to move more naturally. You respond instead of react. You choose instead of comply. You move in ways that feel aligned rather than exhausting.

This isn't ease without effort. It's effort placed where it belongs. It's energy invested in what matters, instead of scattered across what doesn't. It's learning to trust the intelligence of what feels right without needing constant justification.

What comes naturally now is shaped by everything you've learned. It carries wisdom, not avoidance. It carries discernment, not denial.

Today, notice one thing that feels more natural than it used to. Trust it. Let it guide you forward.

May 27th: Holding Complexity With Grace

Life does not simplify just because you heal. In many ways, it becomes more layered. You can feel grateful and sad in the same breath. Strong and tender in the same moment. Certain about some things while deeply unsure about others.

Earlier versions of you may have tried to resolve these contradictions. To pick the "right" feeling. To quiet anything that complicated the story. To force yourself into one clean narrative so you could feel in control again.

But healing does not flatten experience. It expands your capacity to hold it.

Holding complexity is a form of maturity. It means you no longer demand that your emotions line up neatly or make sense to anyone else. You understand that life is not lived in single notes, but in chords. And you are allowed to be a whole chord.

Today, allow two different feelings to coexist without trying to reconcile them. Let them share the space without forcing one to disappear.

May 28th: Standing in Earned Confidence

Confidence now feels different than it once did. Quieter. Less performative. Less concerned with how it appears from the outside.

It shows up as steadiness rather than certainty. As trust in your ability to respond rather than control outcomes. As comfort with not knowing everything and still moving forward anyway.

This confidence wasn't built through affirmation or striving. It was earned through experience. Through being tested. Through making mistakes and staying. Through learning, again and again, that you can meet what arrives.

You no longer need to announce your confidence or defend it. It lives in how you carry yourself. In what you no longer rush to explain.

Today, stand in your confidence without needing to prove it. Let it be felt rather than displayed.

May 29th: When Life Feels Lived In

There's a moment when life stops feeling tentative. You're no longer testing the ground beneath you, wondering if it will hold. You're walking on it.

The days have weight now, but not the heavy kind. The lived-in kind. The kind that comes from showing up repeatedly. Your routines feel familiar again. Your body moves through the world with less hesitation. You recognize your rhythms. You know where you stand more often than you question it.

This doesn't mean everything is easy or settled. It means you belong in your life again. You're not hovering at the edge of it, waiting for permission to enter.

Today, notice one way your life feels lived in rather than fragile. Let yourself appreciate the steadiness of that belonging.

May 30th: Letting Growth Be Ordinary

Growth doesn't always feel triumphant. Most of the time, it feels quiet. Unremarkable. Almost invisible if you're not paying attention.

You don't wake up announcing it. You notice it later, in hindsight. In how you handle an ordinary moment differently than you once did. You pause instead of spiraling. You speak up instead of shrinking. You rest without guilt. You let something go without making a scene about it.

These moments don't ask for recognition. They don't need to be labeled or celebrated. They ask to be lived, again and again, until they become who you are.

Growth that lasts often looks like normalcy reclaimed.

Today, acknowledge one ordinary moment that reflects how you've grown. Let its quietness be proof enough.

May 31st: Early Threads

Some friendships take root early and quietly shape who you become. They grow through shared experiences – playing on the same teams, long afternoons together, first crushes, first heartbreaks, and the small milestones that feel enormous at the time.

These friends witness versions of you that no one else ever will. They know the stories that formed you before you had language for them. The laughter, the tears, the awkwardness, the becoming. Even years later, those shared moments leave a lasting impression.

Time has a way of pulling people in different directions. Lives expand. Paths change. You may fall out of touch, but that doesn't erase what was shared. Some friendships don't need maintenance to remain meaningful. They simply live on, held quietly in the heart.

These early connections remind us where we came from. They carry pieces of our history and help us recognize how far we've grown.

Today, take a moment to remember an early friendship that shaped you. Let gratitude rise for what was shared and for the place that connection still holds in your heart.

June

Staying present while life opens and asks more of you.

June 1st: When Warmth Settles In

There's a difference between warmth that surprises you and warmth that settles. Surprise warmth feels fleeting, almost suspicious. You step outside and wonder how long it will last.

June brings the other kind. The kind that lingers on your skin. That stays even when the sun slips behind a cloud. Warmth that doesn't tease, but arrives with a quiet steadiness.

You notice it in your body before you name it. Your shoulders loosen. Your breath moves more easily. You linger a moment longer at the doorway or step outside without a reason, drawn toward what feels gentle.

Warmth doesn't rush you. It doesn't ask for plans or productivity. It simply invites presence – an easing back into your life, slowly and without effort.

Today, notice where warmth reaches you. Where you soften. Where you still hold. Let yourself receive what's here, just as it is.

June 2nd: Letting the Day Stretch

Some days don't feel as compressed. There's a little more room around the edges. Less of that internal rush to hurry through what's in front of you or to move on before you've really arrived.

And something in you responds. You linger without deciding to. You finish conversations slowly. You let a song play all the way through. You stand still for a few extra moments instead of immediately reaching for the next task. You move through ordinary things without treating them like obstacles to get past.

Not everything needs to be packed tightly to matter. Time doesn't have to be managed to be meaningful. There is room to let moments unfold without pushing them forward.

Today, allow one part of the day to stretch without rushing it. Let yourself move a little more slowly and notice what changes.

June 3rd: The Pull Toward Connection

Sometimes connection feels closer than it did before. Conversations linger. Laughter slips in more easily. There's a subtle shift from wanting distance to wanting company, from withdrawing to staying a little longer than planned.

After a period of careful self-protection, this pull can feel tender. Both inviting and uncertain. Wanting closeness while still aware of your own edges. Not rushing in, not shutting down. Just noticing what it feels like to be drawn toward someone or something again.

Connection doesn't announce itself with certainty. It arrives quietly. In a sentence you don't rehearse. In eye contact that lasts a beat longer. In the choice to stay present rather than step away.

There's no performance required here. No version of yourself to uphold. Just the simple act of showing up as you are.

Today, you might notice where connection hovers nearby. A message left unsent. A conversation waiting. A small opening. You don't have to decide anything yet. Just notice what draws you closer.

June 4th: Staying Present in the Fullness

Fullness can be joyful and overwhelming at the same time. There is more happening. More invitations. More input. More movement. And even when it's good, even when it's wanted, it can still be a lot to hold.

The invitation isn't to pull away from fullness, but to stay present inside it. To enjoy what matters without losing yourself. To notice when your body asks for grounding, even in moments that feel beautiful. Something can be good and still ask for a pause.

Presence keeps fullness from tipping into exhaustion. It allows you to participate without getting swept away. It helps you stay rooted while life moves around you.

Today, pause once in the middle of a full moment. Take one breath. Feel your feet. Let your body know you're still here.

June 5th: When the Body Wants to Play

There are moments when movement slips in without being planned. A stretch while the coffee brews. Bare feet finding the grass. A sway in the kitchen before you realize music is on.

Nothing about it feels like effort. There's no goal attached. No improvement in mind. Just a quiet pull toward motion that feels easy, curious, almost accidental.

It doesn't ask to be organized or impressive. It doesn't care if it counts. It simply shows up as a suggestion, a nudge, a small spark of energy moving through the body.

Sometimes play arrives this way. Not announced. Not justified. Just present.

Today, notice when your body moves without being told. See where it goes when no one is directing it. Let it surprise you.

June 6th: Staying With the Moment

Some moments don't announce themselves.
They pass through quickly – a cool glass of water, light shifting across the floor, a breath that lands a little deeper than the one before it.

You might notice the instinct to move on. To check what's next. To mentally bookmark the moment instead of staying inside it. Not because anything is wrong, but because you're used to motion. Used to keeping pace.

And sometimes, without effort, you pause.
Your shoulders drop. Your breath slows. You stay where you are for a second longer than usual. Nothing changes – except that you're still here.

This is not about holding on.
It's about not rushing past.

Today, notice one small moment as it happens. Let it pass through without reaching for it or stepping away. Just stay close enough to feel it before the day carries you on.

June 7th: Being Here for This Version of Your Life

This moment asks you to show up for the life you have now, not the one you're planning or remembering. Not the life you imagine you'll have once something changes – once you finish the project, fix the relationship, feel more confident, feel more settled. Not the life you replay in your mind, wishing you could return and do differently.

Just this one. This version.

You've grown into this life through experience. Through loss and learning. Through restraint and release. Through the years you held on, and the years you let go. Through small choices that didn't look like much from the outside, but shaped you all the same. You didn't arrive here by accident. You arrived here by continuing.

And still, it can be tempting to act like you're not fully here yet. Like you're waiting for permission. Waiting to feel ready. Waiting for the moment when you're more together, more healed, more certain.

You are already here.

Today, let your attention rest where your feet are. Let this life be the one you stand inside.

June 8th: When the Body Finally Exhales

There is a moment, often unnoticed, when the body stops bracing. Not because everything is suddenly easy, but because something inside recognizes a little more room. A subtle easing. A quiet shift you feel before you understand it.

You might notice it when your jaw relaxes without intention. Or when your shoulders lower on their own. Or when your breath deepens, not because you tried to slow it, but because it finally could. There may be less scanning. Less urgency. Less of that constant readiness held just beneath the surface.

The body remembers what the mind moves past. Long periods of holding it together. Of staying alert. Of being "fine" while something inside stayed tight. Even when you know you are safe, the body learns safety in its own time.

This release doesn't arrive through logic or effort. It comes through sensation. Through letting go without being asked. Through the simple experience of not needing to brace in this moment.

Today, notice where your body eases without instruction, and allow that softness to stay with you a little longer.

June 9th: Letting Yourself Take Up Space

There are moments when you notice yourself showing up a little more fully. Speaking without rehearsing. Laughing without checking the room. Letting your presence land instead of managing how it's received.

It might show up in small ways. Sharing an opinion without apologizing for it. Wearing something that feels like you. Saying what you mean and letting it stand. Nothing dramatic. Just a subtle shift toward being here without shrinking.

For many of us, taking up space once felt risky. Easier to be agreeable. Easier to stay contained. Easier to disappear a little than to risk being seen. Those habits made sense once. They don't have to run the room now.

Taking up space doesn't mean pushing forward or taking over. It means staying. It means not stepping out of yourself mid-moment. It means allowing your presence to be as it is.

Today, notice one small moment where you don't pull back. Let yourself remain where you are.

June 10th: The Vulnerability of Ease

Ease can feel strange when you're not used to it.
When things soften, there's less to push against. Less distraction. Fewer edges to brace yourself on. The quiet can feel almost exposed.

You might notice this when nothing is wrong, yet something stirs. A heaviness in the middle of a good moment. Gratitude brushing up against memory. An emotion that arrives without a clear reason or story.

Ease has a way of uncovering what's been waiting. Not to be fixed or explained, just felt. When urgency loosens its grip, the body and heart speak more clearly. Sometimes what surfaces is relief. Sometimes tenderness. Sometimes both, side by side.

There's no need to harden against this. No need to turn it into a problem.

Today, notice what happens when you let ease stay. When you don't rush to fill the quiet or protect yourself from it. Just remain where you are and feel what it's like to be here without bracing.

June 11th: Where the Light Finds You

There are moments when sunlight feels personal.
Not dramatic. Not overwhelming. Just present.
It warms your skin without asking anything of you. It finds you where you are, whether you're ready or not.

The sun does not pause to assess worthiness.
It doesn't wait for you to feel whole, healed, or certain. It shows up anyway – steady, reliable, offering itself without condition.

To stand in the sun is to be seen without scrutiny.
To be held without explanation.
It reminds you that love does not always arrive as instruction or correction. Sometimes it arrives as warmth. As quiet presence. As light that reaches you even when you're not looking for it.

Faith can feel like this.
Less a belief you perform, more a presence you receive.
A gentle knowing that you are already visible. Already known. Already held by something larger than your effort or understanding.

Today, notice where the light finds you. Let yourself stay there for a moment. Let that warmth remind you that being seen can be gentle - and that love does not require you to hide.

June 12th: At the Water's Edge

The lake is still in the morning.
Not empty. Just settled.

Mist lifts slowly from the surface, the air cool against your skin. The water holds the sky without effort – pale light, drifting clouds, the dark line of trees along the far shore. Nothing insists. Nothing reaches.

You stand close enough to feel the quiet work of it. The way the water receives everything and stays steady. The way it reflects without asking to be understood.

It doesn't need your story.
It doesn't hurry you along.
It offers presence without demand.

There is comfort in that kind of steadiness. A sense of being near something that isn't measuring you or waiting for you to change. Something that can hold what passes over it and remain itself.

You turn back eventually. Life calls you away, as it always does.

But something lingers – the feeling of being seen without effort, of standing before something vast and calm, of being known without words.

Today, carry that steadiness with you. Let it shape how you stand, how you listen, how you move back into your life.

June 13th: Letting Joy Be Simple

Joy does not always need a reason. Sometimes it arrives without ceremony, through the ordinary. Bare feet on warm ground. The smell of something growing. The sound of insects at dusk. A quiet moment that doesn't ask anything of you and doesn't require you to show up as anything other than present.

We often complicate joy. We wait for permission. We look for meaning. We tell ourselves we'll enjoy things later, when they're more earned, more justified, more significant. We turn joy into something we analyze instead of something we feel.

But joy is simplest when it's allowed to be small. When it's not tasked with fixing your life or proving that everything is okay. When it's just a moment of pleasure, passing through, doing what joy does best.

You don't need to make it mean anything. You don't need to document it. You don't need to protect it from the future.

Today, let yourself enjoy one simple pleasure. Let it be quiet. Let it be brief. Let it be enough.

June 14th: Standing Inside the Life You've Built

There is a quiet realization that comes when you notice you are no longer surviving your life. You are living it. Not perfectly. Not without struggle. But with a sense of presence that wasn't always there before.

You still have hard days. Tender moments. Unanswered questions. Things that ache. Things that are unfinished. But there is a feeling of being inside your life rather than watching it from a distance. You are no longer standing on the outside, analyzing every move, waiting for the next thing to go wrong. You are here, participating.

This didn't happen by accident. It happened because you stayed. You chose honesty when it would have been easier to numb or distract. You chose to feel what was real instead of what was convenient. You kept showing up, even when you didn't feel strong, even when you didn't know where it was leading.

Today, stand inside the life you've built and let yourself feel its reality. Let yourself acknowledge what is solid. What is real. What is yours.

June 15th: When You Stop Holding It All

There is a kind of tired that doesn't come from doing too much, but from holding too much. The quiet effort of staying composed. Of being capable. Of keeping things moving even when something inside you is asking to slow down.

It's the tired that comes from being the steady one. The reliable one. The one who notices what needs doing and takes care of it without being asked. Over time, that kind of steadiness can harden into tension you barely register anymore.

Sometimes, without a clear reason, that grip loosens. You breathe a little deeper. You care less about perfect timing or perfect outcomes. You leave something undone and realize the world doesn't fall apart. You begin to trust that not everything requires your constant attention to remain okay.

Letting go doesn't always look dramatic. Often it's subtle. A pause. A softer expectation. A decision not to fix what doesn't need fixing right now.

Today, notice one place where you can loosen your hold. Allow something to remain imperfect. Let yourself step back without explaining why.

June 16th: Belonging Without Performing

There is a kind of belonging that arrives only after you stop trying to earn it.
When you no longer rehearse your words before speaking. When you don't soften yourself to be easier to take. When you don't scan the room, wondering if you're doing it right.

This kind of belonging doesn't announce itself. It settles in slowly.

It grows through ordinary moments. Long conversations. Quiet understanding. Shared laughter and shared silence. It's built not through achievement or effort, but through presence. Through honesty. Through staying exactly as you are and realizing nothing breaks because of it.

This is the belonging that taught me I don't have to work harder to be loved. I don't have to perform wellness, strength, or grace. I don't have to trade my truth for approval.

Sometimes this belonging takes shape through a single person. Someone who stays. Someone who doesn't flinch when you show up as you are. Someone whose steadiness reminds you, again and again, that you are already enough. With them, something in you settles.

Today, notice one moment where you feel that kind of belonging. Where you are seen without effort. Where you are held without conditions. Let it remind you that you were never meant to do this alone.

June 17th: When Confidence Feels Calm

Confidence doesn't always arrive with excitement or certainty. Sometimes it doesn't feel dramatic at all. It feels calm. Grounded. Almost unremarkable in the best way, like a steady hum beneath the surface rather than a rush of adrenaline.

You may notice it in how you respond to challenges. In the way you pause instead of panic. In how little energy you spend replaying conversations or second-guessing your choices. You might feel it in the ease with which you walk away from something that doesn't feel right, without needing to justify or explain yourself afterward.

This confidence isn't loud or flashy. It doesn't need validation. It's the kind that comes from knowing you can handle yourself. From having lived through enough to trust your ability to respond rather than react.

This confidence wasn't built through force or affirmation. It grew through experience. Through showing up. Through making mistakes and learning. Through staying when it would have been easier to abandon yourself.

Today, recognize one moment where confidence shows up quietly. Trust it. Let it guide you without questioning its legitimacy.

June 18th: Letting Others See the Real You

As relationships deepen, you may find yourself sharing more of who you really are. Not the polished version. Not the one that always knows what to say. The honest one. The one with doubts. With tenderness. With a past that shaped you.

This can feel vulnerable. Letting someone see what was once hidden or carefully protected. Old fears can surface. The worry of being misunderstood. And still, there can be relief in it. Like exhaling after holding your breath for a long time. Like resting instead of maintaining an image.

You don't need to reveal everything to everyone. Discernment still matters. But there does need to be enough honesty to stay real. Enough openness that connection doesn't quietly turn into performance.

Today, notice one place where honesty feels possible. Let something true be shared without overexplaining or softening it. See what happens when you allow yourself to be met as you are.

June 19th: The Freedom of Choosing Rest

In a season that celebrates activity, choosing rest can feel almost rebellious. The days are long. The light invites you to keep going. You may feel the pull to say yes simply because there's time, because you "should" take advantage of it, because slowing down feels like wasting something.

But rest is not something you outgrow. It's not a phase you move past once you're stronger or more healed. It's something you learn to choose more intentionally. Something you return to again and again, not because you're failing, but because you're human.

Choosing rest now comes from wisdom, not weakness. It comes from knowing what happens when you don't listen. From understanding that your energy is not infinite, even when the day feels endless.

Today, give yourself permission to rest. Don't earn it. Don't justify it. Don't turn it into recovery for the sake of future productivity. Let rest be enough on its own.

June 20th: Standing in Your Own Authority

Authority does not always look like leadership or certainty. Sometimes it looks like trusting your own judgment. Like honoring your boundaries without apology. Like making decisions that feel right in your body, even when they aren't understood or affirmed by others.

This authority isn't loud. It doesn't demand recognition. It doesn't need to convince anyone. It lives quietly inside you, steady and self-contained. It shows up when you stop asking for permission to be who you are. When you stop outsourcing your knowing.

You've earned this authority through living. Through discernment. Through paying attention. Through learning what aligns and what doesn't, often the hard way.

Today, stand in your own authority. Make one choice from that place of quiet knowing and trust it. Let it be enough that it feels right to you.

June 21st: Living in the Full Light

There is something powerful about the longest day of the year. Light stretches to its fullest expression. Nothing is hidden. Shadows still exist, but they no longer dominate. Everything is visible in a way that feels honest rather than harsh.

You may feel this inside yourself too. A willingness to be seen. A comfort with where you stand. A sense of inhabiting your life fully instead of hovering at the edges. You might notice you're less interested in hiding your flaws or perfecting the story. You're more interested in being present.

This doesn't mean everything is resolved. It means you're here. It means you're no longer waiting to show up until life feels cleaner or simpler.

Today, let yourself live fully in the light. Let yourself be seen in your wholeness. Exactly as you are. Nothing added. Nothing concealed.

June 22nd: When You Stop Arguing With Yourself

There is a particular kind of exhaustion that comes from constantly negotiating with yourself.
Telling yourself you should be over something by now. That you shouldn't feel this way. That other people have it worse, so you should be grateful and move on.

This argument runs quietly in the background of daily life.
While you make coffee. While you drive. While you lie awake at night trying to fall asleep.
It drains more energy than you realize, because it never actually resolves anything. It just keeps you at war with your own experience.

Peace doesn't begin when everything makes sense.
It can begin when you notice that voice and choose not to follow it.
Not because you've figured it all out, but because you're tired of fighting yourself.
Because you're ready to let what's true be true.

There is relief in saying, *this is how I feel today.*
And leaving it there.

Today, notice one moment where you stop arguing with yourself. Let your experience stand on its own, without commentary or correction. Feel the space that opens when you choose peace over persuasion.

June 23rd: Letting Yourself Be As You Are

Summer reveals what winter allowed us to hide. More skin. More light. Fewer layers between you and the world. There is less room to tuck yourself away, less cover for blending into the background.

And you may feel exposed in ways that have nothing to do with your body. Emotions closer to the surface. Old insecurities resurfacing. A heightened awareness of how you speak, move, take up space, or are perceived. When the world feels more visible, so do you.

The instinct may be to adjust. To pull yourself together. To become more acceptable before allowing comfort. To edit what you feel, how you look, or how you show up so it lands more smoothly. Many of us learned early that ease came after adjustment, not before.

But self-acceptance asks something different. It asks you to arrive first, exactly as you are, and decide from there. Not once you've improved. Not once you've figured it out. Now. As is.

Being as you are does not mean you stop growing. It means you stop postponing your presence until you feel worthy of it.

Today, allow yourself to exist as you are in one moment. Don't correct. Don't prepare. Don't apologize. Let that be enough.

June 24th: Making Peace With Your Pace

There is a pace you move at when no one is watching. When you're not trying to keep up. When you're not anticipating judgment or comparison. When you're not explaining yourself.

This pace has always been there. You can feel it when you walk alone. When you cook without distraction. When you move through a day that isn't crowded with expectation. It's steady. It's responsive. It's honest.

But many of us learned to ignore it. We learned to move faster than felt natural. To override fatigue. To push through signals that asked for rest or pause. We were taught that slowing down meant falling behind, that ease meant laziness, that our natural rhythm was an inconvenience.

Self-acceptance grows when you stop treating your pace as a problem to solve. When you stop measuring it against someone else's capacity or speed. When you let your body set the tempo instead of your fear.

You don't need to justify your pace. You only need to listen to it.

Today, notice the speed that feels most honest in your body. Let one thing take exactly as long as it needs to. Choose to honor that rhythm, even if it's quieter than the world around you.

June 25th: Accepting the Body You Live In

Your body has been with you through everything. The moments you remember clearly and the ones you survived without fully understanding. It carried you through joy and shock, through holding and letting go, through seasons you never thought you'd get through.

It adapted when it needed to. It learned patterns to keep you functioning. It held stress when there was no other option. It protected you in ways that may not have been comfortable, but were necessary at the time.

Acceptance does not mean loving your body every day. It does not mean pretending the relationship has always been easy. It means recognizing its effort. Its intelligence. Its loyalty. It means seeing your body not as something that failed you, but as something that stayed.

Your body is not a project. It is not an object to perfect. It is a witness. It remembers what you lived through and how hard you tried.

Today, offer your body one quiet moment of appreciation. A hand on your chest. A deep breath. A gentle stretch. No demands. No requests for change. Just acknowledgment.

June 26th: Releasing the Self That Survived

There are versions of yourself you worked hard to maintain. The one who didn't need help. The one who kept the peace. The one who stayed composed no matter what was happening inside. The one who handled it, whatever "it" was, without letting it show.

These versions were not mistakes. They were responses. They were intelligent adaptations to the seasons you were in. They kept you functioning. They kept you moving forward when stopping wasn't an option.

But what protected you then may constrain you now.

You don't need these versions in the same way anymore. You don't need to stay braced. You don't need to keep proving your resilience. You don't need to be the strong one at the cost of being real.

Self-acceptance allows you to thank who you were without requiring you to remain her. It lets you honor the role she played while choosing something gentler for the life you're living now.

Today, notice one role you can begin to release. Do it softly. Without drama. Let yourself change without needing to explain why.

June 27th: Staying With Discomfort

There are moments when discomfort rises and every instinct tells you to leave yourself. To distract. To scroll. To numb. To analyze the feeling until it becomes something else. To turn against your own experience by telling yourself you shouldn't feel this way in the first place.

Leaving yourself often feels efficient. It promises quick relief. But it comes at a cost. Each time you abandon your inner experience, even briefly, something learns that discomfort is unsafe and must be escaped.

Staying is a choice you learn slowly. It doesn't come from force or toughness. It comes from trust built over time. Trust that feelings move. Trust that you are not fragile. Trust that you can sit inside discomfort without being consumed by it.

Staying looks simple, but it's not easy. You sit with the feeling. You breathe instead of bracing. You notice where it lives in your body. You remind yourself, quietly, I am allowed to feel this and remain intact. I don't need to fix it to survive it.

This is self-acceptance in action.

Today, practice staying with yourself through one uncomfortable moment. Keep it small. Offer patience instead of criticism. Let presence do what resistance never could.

June 28th: Belonging to Yourself

Belonging is often something we look for outside ourselves. In approval. In acceptance. In being understood or chosen. We learn early that belonging seems to come from fitting in, from being wanted, from being seen in the "right" way.

But there is a deeper belonging that forms when you stop leaving yourself. When you stay present even when you're imperfect, uncertain, or hurting. When you don't disappear at the first sign of discomfort. When you don't withdraw your own care because you're disappointed in yourself.

This belonging is quiet and steady. It doesn't announce itself. It doesn't depend on circumstances or validation. It grows through returning to yourself, one honest moment at a time. Each time you choose to stay, something inside you relaxes and thinks, I'm not alone in here anymore.

You don't need to earn this belonging. You don't need to prove yourself worthy of it. You already belong.

Today, let yourself belong to yourself fully. No conditions. No improvement plan. Just presence. Let that be enough.

June 29th: Living Without the Inner Editor

There is a subtle shift that happens when you stop monitoring yourself so closely. When the inner editor quiets. When you're no longer narrating everything you say or do, wondering how it sounds, how it looks, how it lands.

You may notice moments where you simply respond instead of calculating. Where laughter comes out unfiltered. Where you speak before the second-guessing kicks in. Where silence feels natural instead of something you need to fill or explain. These moments can feel strangely spacious, as if you've stepped out of a cramped room you didn't realize you were living in.

This isn't carelessness. It's relief. It's what happens when you trust yourself enough to stop managing every interaction. When you believe you don't need constant oversight to be acceptable.

Living without the constant need to edit yourself creates space. Space to be present. Space to be real. Space to feel your life instead of managing it from the sidelines.

Today, notice one moment where you move or speak without editing yourself. Let that freedom register in your body. Let yourself remember what it feels like to be unguarded.

June 30th: Standing in Self-Acceptance

As the month closes, there is no need for review or judgment. No need to tally progress or measure how much you've healed. Healing doesn't move in straight lines, and self-acceptance doesn't arrive on a schedule.

Instead, there's an invitation to stand where you are and notice what feels different. How you speak to yourself when something goes wrong. How you treat your body on an ordinary day. How quickly you find your way back when you notice you've drifted.

Self-acceptance doesn't arrive all at once. It settles in quietly, through small decisions to stay rather than leave, to soften rather than criticize, to listen instead of override. It shows up in the way you hold yourself when no one else is watching.

You are not finished. You are becoming. And you are allowed to stand here, exactly as you are.

Today, pause and notice the steadiness beneath you. Let yourself recognize this moment as a place you're allowed to stand.

July

Learning how to live fully without abandoning yourself.

July 1st: Living in the Heat

July arrives without hesitation. The air is thick. The sun is bold. There is no subtlety left in the season. Spring's gentleness is gone. What's here now is direct, undeniable, and fully present.

You feel it immediately. In skin that warms faster than you expect. In sweat that appears without asking permission. In the way your body responds before your mind has time to narrate what's happening. Heat brings you out of abstraction and straight into sensation. There's no distance between you and the experience.

Heat asks for honesty. You can't pretend you're not affected. You can't power through it without consequence. You adjust. You slow down. You drink more water. You seek shade. You listen more closely to what your body needs instead of overriding it out of habit or pride.

This kind of awareness isn't limitation. It's freedom. It's being responsive instead of resistant. It's letting your body be the authority instead of something you manage from a distance.

Today, notice how your body responds to the heat. Where you soften. Where you slow. Where you need more care. Honor what it asks of you without judgment or negotiation.

July 2nd: Choosing Freedom Over Familiarity

Freedom doesn't always feel comfortable at first. Often, it feels disorienting. It asks you to step out of routines and patterns that once kept you safe, even if they no longer fit the person you are now. Familiarity has gravity. It pulls at you quietly, reminding you how predictable it can be to stay the same.

You may notice moments where you stand at a small crossroads. You could choose the familiar response, the familiar role, the familiar way of coping. Or you could choose something different. The familiar still calls to you. It always will. Familiarity isn't wrong. It just isn't always true anymore.

Now, you recognize the difference between habit and alignment. Between comfort that soothes and comfort that confines. You can feel when a choice comes from fear of change versus trust in yourself.

Freedom grows when you choose yourself intentionally, not impulsively. When you pause long enough to ask, Does this still serve who I am becoming? And then listen for the answer without trying to talk yourself out of it.

Today, notice one place where you choose freedom over familiarity. Let yourself feel the difference in your body. The openness. The steadiness. The quiet relief of choosing what's true.

July 3rd: Letting the Body Lead

There are times when you feel drawn back into your body. Into sensation. Into movement that doesn't need to be explained or justified. The body becomes less managed and more present.

Your body remembers joy before words. It remembers what it feels like to move without being watched. To stretch without a goal. To rest without guilt. To exist without correction. Long before you learned how to evaluate yourself, your body knew how to be here.

Letting the body lead can feel unfamiliar if you've spent years living from the neck up. If you've relied on thinking, planning, or controlling as a way to stay safe. But the body doesn't rush. It doesn't perform. It responds honestly to what's happening.

Embodiment is not performance. It's presence. It's allowing sensation to guide you instead of overriding it with expectation or judgment.

Today, let your body lead one small choice. When to rest. When to move. What feels good. Follow without overthinking it. Let that trust build quietly.

July 4th: Defining Your Own Freedom

Independence is often framed as separation. As standing alone. As needing nothing. As proving you can handle everything by yourself. That version of freedom can look strong on the outside, but feel lonely or exhausting on the inside.

Real freedom feels different. It feels like choice. Like honesty. Like knowing when to say yes and when to say no without fear of losing yourself or someone else. It feels like being able to stay connected without being controlled. Like resting without guilt. Like speaking truth without bracing for fallout.

You are no longer defining freedom by escape or rebellion. You are defining it by alignment. By what allows you to live in integrity with your body, your values, and your limits. Freedom becomes less about breaking away and more about coming home to yourself.

Today, reflect on what freedom means to you now. Not in theory, but in sensation. Notice how it feels in your body when you imagine living in alignment. Let that feeling guide you.

July 5th: The Confidence of Being Comfortable

There is a confidence that comes from comfort. Not the loud, performative kind. The settled kind. The kind that doesn't need to announce itself or seek approval. It shows up quietly, in how you move through your day without constantly adjusting.

You may notice yourself being less self-conscious. Less aware of how you're being perceived. Less inclined to check, correct, or compare. You inhabit your own skin more fully. You take up space without apologizing for it. You let yourself be seen without managing the outcome.

This confidence wasn't built overnight. It was built slowly. Through acceptance. Through listening. Through choosing differently again and again. Through learning that you don't need to earn comfort by becoming someone else.

Today, notice one moment where you feel comfortable being yourself. Let it register. Let your body remember that comfort can be safe, and that confidence can feel this gentle.

July 6th: Playing Without Permission

Play often disappears quietly in adulthood. There's no announcement when it leaves. No clear moment when you decide you're done with it. It simply gets crowded out by productivity, responsibility, and restraint. By the pressure to be useful. By the belief that everything needs a purpose to be worthwhile.

And then, sometimes, play finds its way back in. Gently. Without explanation. Laughter comes more easily. Time loosens its grip. Moments unfold that don't need to lead anywhere or become anything. You find yourself doing something simply because it feels good, not because it's efficient or impressive.

Play is not frivolous. It is restorative. It gives the nervous system a chance to soften. It reminds your body that joy doesn't have to be justified or earned. That pleasure can exist without productivity attached to it.

Many of us learned to wait for permission to enjoy ourselves. To make sure everything else was handled first. To be responsible before being playful. But play doesn't thrive under rules. It thrives under freedom.

Today, allow yourself one moment of play. Keep it small. Keep it honest. Don't explain it. Don't earn it. Let joy arrive without asking permission.

July 7th: Trusting the Life You're Living

There is a point when you stop waiting for life to begin. When you realize it has been happening all along, even in the moments you thought were just preparation or survival. Even in the years that felt messy, uncertain, or unfinished.

You trust yourself more now. Not because everything is certain, but because you know you can respond. You've handled things you never imagined you could. You've adapted. You've stayed. You've learned how to meet life as it comes instead of needing it to be predictable first.

This trust doesn't feel flashy. It feels steady. It shows up in how you move through uncertainty without panic. In how you don't immediately assume you're doing it wrong. In how you stay present instead of bracing for collapse.

This trust creates a quiet confidence. One that doesn't need to prove anything or rush toward the next milestone. One that rests in the understanding that you are already living your life, not waiting on the sidelines.

Today, pause and trust the life you're living. Exactly as it is. Let yourself believe that you're not behind, and that nothing essential is missing from this moment.

July 8th: When You're No Longer Bracing

There are moments when you suddenly notice what's missing. The tightness in your chest. The constant readiness for something to go wrong. The feeling that you need to stay one step ahead of life in order to survive it.

You don't remember exactly when this changed. There wasn't a single breakthrough or dramatic shift. It happened quietly, over time. Through choosing yourself when it mattered. Through staying present instead of escaping. Through learning, again and again, that you can handle what comes without staying in constant defense.

Summer brings this awareness into the body. You sit outside and realize you're not scanning for exits. You laugh without watching yourself. You breathe without holding anything back. There's a sense of ease that doesn't need to be explained or monitored.

This is not carelessness. It's not naïveté. It is trust. The kind that settles in when your nervous system learns that the threat has passed, and that you don't have to stay on guard to stay safe.

Today, notice one moment where you are no longer bracing. Let yourself rest in that ease. Let your body remember that this, too, is allowed.

July 9th: The Freedom of Choice

Choice feels different now. It's no longer about proving independence or rebelling against expectations. It's about honesty. About listening instead of reacting. About choosing from alignment rather than obligation.

You notice the space between impulse and action. That brief pause where you can check in with yourself and ask what you actually want, instead of doing what's familiar or automatic. In that pause, you reclaim your agency.

This freedom isn't loud. It doesn't announce itself or demand recognition. It lives in small, steady decisions that reflect who you are now. In the yes that feels clean. In the no that doesn't require apology. In the choice to move at your own pace.

Freedom, at this stage, is less about escape and more about self-respect.

Today, pause before one choice. Breathe. Listen inward. Let the decision come from truth rather than habit, and notice how that feels in your body.

July 10th: Being at Home in Your Body

Summer invites you fully into your body. Heat, movement, water, bare skin. There is less hiding, physically and emotionally. The body becomes less something you manage from a distance and more something you inhabit.

You may notice how different this feels from earlier seasons of your life. Times when your body felt like a problem to solve, a thing to control, or a place you tried to escape from altogether. Times when listening felt risky, or when sensation brought up too much to hold.

Now, something has shifted. There is more listening. More respect. More willingness to be where you are without immediately trying to change it. You notice sensations without labeling them as good or bad. You respond instead of overriding.

This isn't about perfection. It's not about loving every part of your body every day. It's about presence. About relationship. About allowing your body to be a home instead of a battleground.

Today, notice one moment where you feel at home in your body. Maybe it's in movement. Maybe it's in stillness. Maybe it's in water, warmth, or breath. Let it stay a little longer.

July 11th: Letting Yourself Be Seen in the Light

July light is direct.
It shows what's here without much buffering. Colors are sharper. Edges clearer. There's less room to hide behind shadow or blur.

Being seen this clearly can feel vulnerable. You may notice the old urge to perform. To polish. To present only the most acceptable version of yourself. To manage how you're received so nothing feels too exposed or uncertain. These habits often come from a time when being fully real didn't feel safe.

But you've learned something important. You don't need to earn your place by being impressive. You don't need to change yourself to belong. You don't need to dim or sharpen who you are to make it easier for others to take in.

You belong by being real.

Today, allow yourself to be seen as you are in one small moment. Say what you mean without softening it. Let your face show what you feel. Stay present without editing yourself. Let visibility be something you practice, not something you survive.

July 12th: Joy Without Holding Back

Joy feels different when you stop holding it at arm's length. When you don't dampen it to stay safe. When you let yourself laugh fully, feel deeply, enjoy without reservation or apology.

Many of us learned to temper joy. To keep it controlled. To stay alert even in good moments, as if too much happiness might invite loss. This kind of restraint can feel protective, but it also keeps joy from ever fully landing.

Letting yourself feel joy doesn't mean forgetting what you've been through. It means trusting yourself enough to live now. It means knowing that you can hold both pleasure and memory without needing to shut either down.

Joy is not naïve. It is courageous. It requires presence. It asks you to be open instead of guarded.

Today, let yourself experience joy fully in one moment. Let it fill your body. Let it move through you without being managed. Notice how it feels to stay open.

July 13th: Letting Joy Be Simple

Some people meet the world through intensity. Through texture, sound, color, feeling. Joy doesn't arrive for them as an abstract idea – it arrives through the body. Through fascination. Through moments that feel absorbing, specific, alive.

This kind of joy is often quiet. Focused. It doesn't perform or explain itself. It doesn't rush to share its reasons. It simply exists – honest and whole – in the moment it's being felt.

You may have learned to soften this joy. To make it smaller. To worry about whether it makes sense to others. But joy does not need translation to be real. Delight does not need permission to matter.

There is wisdom in allowing what lights you up, even if it looks different than what lights up the room around you. There is strength in honoring the way you feel, the way you notice, the way you love what you love.

Today, let one simple joy take up space. Follow it without questioning. Stay with it without rushing. Let yourself experience the fullness of being exactly who you are – without apology.

July 14th: Standing in Who You Are Now

There is a quiet confidence that comes from knowing who you are. Not because you've arrived somewhere perfect or finished, but because you've stopped abandoning yourself along the way.

You trust your limits now. You honor your needs. You allow yourself to change without needing to explain every shift. You're less interested in being consistent for others and more committed to being honest with yourself.

This confidence doesn't announce itself. It doesn't seek validation. It shows up in how you move through the world. In the boundaries you hold. In the choices you make. In the way you no longer rush to justify your existence.

Today, stand confidently in who you are now. Let yourself take up space in your own life. Let that be enough.

July 15th: When You Notice How Far You've Come

Sometimes it happens in the middle of an ordinary moment. You're standing at the sink. Walking outside. Pausing before responding to something that once would have pulled you under.

And you realize you're not reacting the way you used to. Your body doesn't flood the same way. Your thoughts don't spiral as fast. There is space now. Choice. A steadiness that wasn't there before. You don't feel the need to explain yourself or rush to make things okay.

This realization doesn't arrive with pride or fanfare. It arrives quietly, like a knowing that settles into your chest and stays there. A gentle recognition that something fundamental has shifted.

You've come a long way, even if you didn't notice it happening.

Today, pause and acknowledge one moment that shows how far you've come. Let yourself receive that truth without minimizing it.

July 16th: The Freedom of Saying No

There are times when invitations multiply. Gatherings. Expectations. Opportunities to say yes simply because it feels easier than pausing to check in. Because everyone else is going. Because declining might feel awkward or disappointing.

You may notice the familiar pull to say yes automatically. To keep things smooth. To avoid tension. For a long time, saying yes may have felt like the safest option – even when it cost you something quietly, internally.

And then, something begins to shift.

You pause a little longer before answering. You notice how your body responds. The word *no* doesn't carry the same charge it once did. There is less justification, less urgency to explain.

This no doesn't come from defensiveness or withdrawal. It comes from recognizing your limits and respecting them. From sensing when honesty is kinder than resentment. Kinder than showing up while slowly disappearing from yourself.

Saying no is not rejection. It is not a failure of generosity or love. It is an act of clarity. And clarity allows your yes to mean something again.

Today, notice one place where you pause before agreeing. Let yourself listen for what's true.

July 17th: Letting Yourself Be Seen

Some changes arrive quietly. They don't announce themselves or ask to be noticed. They show up through small choices that slowly change how you live inside yourself.

You may begin to notice where you've been editing or managing who you are. How you present yourself. How much effort goes into appearing acceptable or put together. Sometimes this shows up in how you wear your natural hair or how much you cover or correct. Other times, it's less visible – in the feelings you temper or the parts of yourself you keep out of view.

Over time, this kind of managing can feel normal. Necessary, even. As if parts of you need adjustment before they're allowed to exist freely.

Healing gently interrupts that pattern. As layers fall away, there's a growing awareness of where hiding still lives. Where energy is spent performing instead of simply being. Letting something remain unaltered can feel vulnerable – a quiet choice to stop smoothing yourself into acceptability and allow what's natural to take up space.

This isn't really about appearance. It's about presence. When performance softens, truth has room to breathe. When hiding loosens, belonging becomes possible.

Today, notice one place you allow yourself to remain unaltered.

July 18th: The Joy of Not Overthinking

There are moments when the mind goes quiet on its own. You stop replaying conversations. Stop anticipating what's next. Stop narrating your every move as if you're being evaluated.

You might notice it in laughter that comes easily and surprises you.
In movement that feels fluid instead of controlled.
In time that passes without being counted or measured.

These moments often arrive without effort – slipping in when you are present enough to receive them.

This ease is not accidental.
It is not luck.

It is the result of learning to trust yourself in the moment. Of knowing that you do not need constant mental oversight to stay safe or do things "right." Of letting your body lead without interruption.

When the mind rests, joy has room to breathe.

Today, notice one moment when you are not overthinking. Stay there just a bit longer. Let your body memorize how it feels to be unguarded.

July 19th: What Brings You to Life

Some people teach you how to live simply by the way they enjoy being alive. Big laughs. Easy affection. Music turned up. Long conversations. Showing up fully, even in ordinary moments.

You remember this kind of joy in the body. The way laughter takes over without restraint. The comfort of being pulled into a hug that leaves no room for doubt. The feeling of a song filling the space and everyone in it at once. Nothing rushed. Nothing withheld.

This kind of living doesn't chase happiness. It recognizes it when it arrives. It knows how to linger. It understands that pleasure isn't frivolous – it's connective. It's how people gather. How memories are made. How love moves through a room.

Enjoyment, at its best, is generous. It invites others in. It reminds you that being here is something to participate in, not manage or postpone.

Today, notice what brings you to life. Music that opens your chest. Time with people who feel easy. A moment of laughter that needs no explanation. Let yourself receive it fully.

July 20th: Choosing Yourself

There are moments in life that feel like milestones, even when nothing outwardly dramatic happens. You wake up in the same body, in the same circumstances, but something inside you knows this season is different. The shift isn't loud. It's felt more than seen.

You remember earlier versions of yourself who didn't yet know how to stay. Who coped by leaving their body, their truth, their needs. They did what they knew how to do. They kept you going when the path forward wasn't clear.

Growth doesn't erase those versions. It honors them. It recognizes how hard they worked to keep you alive until you learned another way. There is tenderness in that recognition. Gratitude, even.

Standing here now, you are not finished. But you are present. You know how to listen to yourself. How to pause when something hurts. How to choose care over escape, honesty over approval, staying over running. These are not small shifts. They are foundational.

This moment is not about time passing. It's about awareness. About being awake inside your own life.

You don't need a date or a marker to name it. Your presence is the evidence.

Today, honor the year you chose yourself. Let that be enough.

July 21st: Belonging to This Version of Yourself

There are versions of life you rush through, already leaning toward what comes next. You tell yourself this part is temporary. That real living will begin later, once something changes or settles.
And then there are versions you stop moving past.

You belong to this version of yourself. The one who knows when to engage and when to rest. When to speak and when to listen. When to play and when to be still. The one who doesn't measure growth by how quickly you outgrow the present.

Belonging here doesn't mean you're finished evolving. It means you're no longer treating the present as something to endure. You're allowing it to inform you. To shape you. To matter.

You don't need to hurry past this version of yourself. You don't need to use it as a stepping stone to something else.

Today, let yourself belong to where you are. Let this version hold you, without needing to push you forward.

July 22nd: An Ordinary Day

Being on a healing journey can quietly create its own kind of pressure.
The sense that you should be noticing something. Learning something. Moving forward in some visible way.

But not every day asks for healing to be the focus.

Some days are meant to be lived without attention on the process at all.
You wake up. You move through familiar moments. You eat, rest, respond. Nothing opens. Nothing closes.

This, too, is healing.
Not because anything is happening, but because you are not trying to make something happen.

Today, let the day be ordinary. Let the absence of effort be part of what restores you.

July 23rd: Letting the Pace Normalize

After moments of significance, there can be a temptation to keep reaching. To stay heightened. To turn meaning into momentum. To hold onto intensity as proof that something mattered.

But there is another way things settle. After change, the body adjusts. The rhythm becomes livable again. What was intense begins to integrate. What was new finds its place. Life doesn't lose meaning when it becomes familiar – it becomes sustainable.

You don't need to maintain a heightened version of yourself to honor what you've learned. You don't need to keep proving that growth is happening. Growth that lasts settles into your nervous system. It becomes part of how you move through ordinary days.

You are allowed to return to a pace that feels human. A pace that includes rest, repetition, and steadiness without the fear of losing something important.

Today, let your pace normalize. Let things steady. Trust that what matters doesn't disappear just because life grows quieter.

July 24th: Living the Lessons, Not Preaching Them

Growth doesn't need an audience. The most meaningful changes rarely do. They don't announce themselves or ask to be recognized. They simply show up, again and again, in how you live.

You may notice how little you feel compelled to explain your choices now. How comfortable you are letting your life speak for itself. You don't need to convince anyone you've changed. You're more interested in staying aligned than being understood.

You've learned that wisdom is quieter than performance. That truth doesn't need embellishment. That integrity often looks ordinary from the outside.

Today, live one lesson without articulating it. Hold a boundary. Choose rest. Speak honestly. Or stay silent when that feels more honest. Let the lesson live in your actions, not your explanations.

July 25th: When Balance Feels Like Freedom

There was a time when balance felt like restriction. Like holding back. Like saying no to things you wanted in order to be "good," responsible, or in control. Balance felt like a rule imposed from the outside, not a choice made from within.

Now, it feels different. It feels like freedom. Like knowing when to stop without resentment. Like leaving something early and feeling relief instead of guilt. Like choosing less and discovering that less can actually be enough.

This balance wasn't handed to you. It wasn't taught in a single moment. You earned it by listening. By noticing what drained you and what sustained you. By paying attention to the quiet signals that told you when enough was enough. By trusting those signals even when they went against expectation.

Balance, now, is not about restriction. It's about self-respect.

Today, choose balance in one place. Let yourself stop when it feels right. Let the choice feel liberating instead of limiting.

July 26th: The Confidence of Staying Soft

There is strength in staying soft in a world that often rewards hardness. A world that praises endurance, stoicism, and the ability to push through at any cost. Softness, in contrast, is often misunderstood. Mistaken for fragility. Dismissed as weakness.

But softness allows feeling. Listening. Adjusting. It lets you respond instead of react. It keeps you connected to yourself and to others in ways that hardness never could. Softness is what allows nuance. It's what keeps your heart open even after you've learned how much it can hurt.

You may have once equated strength with survival alone. With gritting your teeth. With getting through no matter what it cost you internally. That kind of strength kept you going when you needed it to. But it doesn't have to define you anymore.

Now you know better.

Staying soft doesn't mean you lack boundaries. It means you know when to bend and when to stand. It means you can feel without being overtaken. It means you trust yourself to handle life without armoring up first.

Today, notice one place where softness supports you rather than weakens you. Let it be a source of confidence, not doubt.

July 27th: Choosing Presence Over Noise

There is always noise. Activity. Constant input. Things to attend to, respond to, keep up with. It's easy to feel pulled in many directions at once, your attention scattered before you realize it.

But you've learned how to choose presence instead. How to stay connected to yourself even when things feel loud. How to turn inward without disappearing. How to listen for what actually matters beneath layers of stimulation and expectation.

This choice doesn't come from withdrawal. It comes from clarity. From knowing that not every sound deserves your attention. That not every invitation requires a response. That your presence carries the most weight when it's intentional.

Choosing presence is how you stay anchored. It's how you remain yourself in the middle of motion.

Today, choose presence in one noisy moment. Take a breath. Feel your body. Let that awareness settle you where you are.

July 28th: Living Without Needing to Be Understood

There is relief in letting go of the need to be understood by everyone. Relief in realizing you don't need to translate yourself into something more palatable. You don't need to shrink your truth or overexplain your choices so they make sense to others.

You begin to trust that the right people will meet you where you are. And that those who don't are not a problem to solve. You stop exhausting yourself trying to manage perception. You let misunderstandings exist without rushing to fix them.

This doesn't make you careless. It makes you free. Free to speak honestly. Free to live according to what's true for you. Free to let your life unfold without constant commentary.

This freedom creates space. Space for authenticity to breathe. Space for relationships that don't require constant clarification. Space for you to simply be.

Today, live one truth without needing it to be validated. Let it stand on its own. Trust that you don't need universal understanding to be real.

July 29th: Letting the Moment Be

There was a time when you tried to hold on tightly to good moments. To photograph them. To replay them. To make sure they didn't slip away unnoticed. Capturing felt like a way to protect yourself from loss.

Now, something has softened. You don't feel the same urgency to preserve or document everything. You trust the moment to live where it belongs, inside you. You let the evening unfold without checking the time. You laugh without wondering how long it will last. You feel joy without immediately bracing for its end.

You've learned that presence doesn't require proof. That memory doesn't need constant reinforcement. That some moments are meant to be felt fully and then released.

This is presence without fear. Joy without guarding. Experience without grasping.

Today, let one moment pass through you without trying to hold on to it. Let it come. Let it go. Trust that it leaves its mark anyway.

July 30th: Living Without the Countdown

As summer stretches on, there's often an unspoken countdown. How many weeks left. How many weekends remain. How quickly it all seems to move once you start measuring it.

But you've learned something important. Life isn't meant to be rushed through or tracked in advance. It's meant to be inhabited. Meant to be lived from the inside rather than monitored from a distance.

When you stop counting, you notice more. You feel more. You stop trying to get ahead of joy before it disappears. You let the season be what it is, not what it's about to become.

You don't need to anticipate the ending to appreciate where you are. You don't need to hurry beauty before it fades.

Today, release the countdown. Stay fully where you are. Let the moment be enough without measuring how much of it remains.

July 31st: The Freedom of Floating

Out on the water, effort softens.
You're not rushing anywhere. You're not fixing your balance – just responding to it. Small shifts. Gentle corrections. A steady rhythm that doesn't need commentary.

Floating teaches you this kind of freedom.
Not the dramatic kind that breaks away, but the quiet kind that trusts what holds you. The board stays steady because you let it. The water carries you because you stop fighting its movement.

You feel the difference in your body.
Shoulders drop. Breath deepens. Thoughts loosen their grip. There's nothing to prove out here. No pace to match. Just you, upright and supported, moving because you choose to.

This is what it feels like to trust without bracing. To stay present without effort. To let yourself be held while still participating in your own direction.

Today, let yourself float a little more than you push. Notice where balance comes when you stop trying to control it. Let that freedom carry you.

August

Learning how to stay present when life feels full and bright.

August 1st: When Things Settle In

Some experiences don't arrive in bursts. They settle in and stay. They linger through your days, following you quietly, asking something of you whether you planned to answer or not.

Your body often notices before your mind does. Movement slows. Energy comes in waves instead of surges. There's less urgency now, less desire to rush or prove. You may find yourself pausing more naturally, leaving space between tasks, listening more closely to what your body is asking for.

This stretch doesn't reward pushing. It doesn't respond well to forcing or powering through. It asks for adjustment. For attention. For care.

There is wisdom in responding rather than resisting. In letting yourself soften into what is, instead of fighting against it.

Today, notice how your body responds when things feel sustained. Where you tire more quickly. Where you need rest, nourishment, or space. Allow yourself to respond with care, rather than resistance.

August 2nd: Learning to Savor

There is a sweetness that only reveals itself when you slow down. Moments feel more complete when you let them stand on their own, without needing to turn them into something useful or impressive.

Savoring is a practice. One many of us were never taught. We learned how to move on quickly, how to rush through pleasure, how to stay slightly guarded even in good moments. Sometimes we hurry because we're afraid joy will disappear if we look at it too closely.

But savoring doesn't make joy fragile. It makes it felt.

When you linger, when you stay, when you allow yourself to fully experience what's good without reaching ahead, something settles in your body. The moment doesn't just pass through you. It lands.

Today, slow down long enough to savor one simple moment fully. Let it be unproductive. Let it be quiet. Let it fill you without asking anything in return.

August 3rd: Telling the Truth About Your Energy

There are moments when things become clearer. What drains you stands out. What nourishes you is easier to recognize. You feel less willing to pretend you have more energy than you do.

You may notice a growing resistance to overriding fatigue or forcing enthusiasm. A quieter refusal to say yes just to keep things moving. This isn't laziness or disengagement. It's honesty. It's your body speaking plainly after a long stretch of effort and growth.

Your energy is not meant to be spent everywhere. It's meant to be invested. Offered where it matters, where it feels aligned, where it gives something back instead of taking everything.

Listening to your energy is an act of self-respect.

Today, tell the truth about your energy. Notice where it rises and where it dips. Let that truth guide one choice, even if it means doing less than you planned.

August 4th: Letting Things Ripen

Not everything is ready yet. Some things still need time. More space. More quiet attention.

You don't have to rush what's still forming. Forcing clarity too soon often flattens what needs room to deepen. Timing matters, and readiness can't be manufactured without losing something essential.

You can offer yourself the same grace. Not every question needs an answer right now. Not every decision needs to be made. Not every part of you has to know what comes next.

There is value in waiting without anxiety. In trusting that understanding takes shape in its own time.

Today, notice one thing in your life that is still forming. A feeling. A relationship. A decision. Allow it the time it needs without trying to move it along before it's ready.

August 5th: Resting Without Apology

Rest doesn't always arrive as refreshment. Sometimes it comes heavier. Deeper. Less about feeling energized and more about feeling steadied.

You may feel called to nap. To sit quietly. To cancel something you thought you should be able to handle. To do less than you planned – not because you failed, but because your body is asking for care.

This kind of rest isn't indulgent. It's responsive. It's what the body asks for after sustained effort, engagement, and growth. It's maintenance, not escape.

You don't need to justify this rest. You don't need to explain it away or promise you'll make up for it later.

Today, rest without apology. Let your body receive what it's asking for. Let rest be enough on its own.

August 6th: The Wisdom of Staying Put

There is wisdom in staying where you are instead of always reaching for what's next. Right now, there are moments when nothing is required of you except presence.

You sit. You watch. You notice what's been growing quietly all along. The things that didn't announce themselves. The shifts that happened slowly, without fanfare.

Staying put doesn't mean stagnation. It doesn't mean giving up or falling behind. It means honoring what's here before moving on. Letting yourself fully inhabit the moment you're in instead of treating it like a waiting room.

There is richness in staying long enough to see what reveals itself.

Today, stay with one moment without trying to move on from it. Let yourself be where you are. Let that be enough.

August 7th: The Ease of Being Yourself

Some people carry a natural ease with them. They enter a space and bring energy without trying to. Conversation flows. Laughter comes easily. There is a sense of comfort in how they show up, as if they trust themselves enough to be present without second-guessing every move.

This ease doesn't mean everything feels simple on the inside. Often, it's the result of paying attention over time. Of learning when to lean in and when to step back. Of discovering that openness and discernment can exist together.

There is a way of loving that is generous without being boundless. Warm without being self-sacrificing. It knows how to offer connection while still honoring personal limits. This kind of presence feels honest rather than performative. Grounded rather than loud.

It takes quiet confidence to live this way. To let yourself be seen without needing approval. To speak when it feels true and stay silent when it doesn't. To belong to yourself first, and let everything else grow from there.

Today, notice this kind of ease – in someone you admire or in moments when you feel it within yourself. Let it remind you that belonging begins with being at home in yourself.

August 8th: When the Days Ask Less of You

There are days that seem to ask very little. Even when life continues around you, something underneath it all feels quieter, less demanding.

You may notice an internal shift on days like this. Less urgency. Less drive to accomplish or explain. A sense that simply being present is enough. That you don't need to fill the space with effort in order for the day to count.

If you've spent years equating worth with productivity, this can feel unfamiliar. Even uncomfortable. You might notice the reflex to justify your existence through action. But there is wisdom in these quieter days.

They remind you that you do not need to perform your life in order to live it. That presence carries value on its own.

Today, allow the day to ask less of you. Don't rush to fill the space. Notice what remains when you stop pushing.

August 9th: Carrying What's Been Revealed

Over time, life shows you things. About your energy. Your limits. Your capacity for joy, rest, and honesty. These insights don't arrive as bold statements or final conclusions. They show up quietly, through lived experience.

You may feel them more than you can articulate them. A sense of what you want more of. A clearer knowing of what no longer fits. A recognition of where you feel most like yourself and where you feel depleted.

These truths don't need immediate action. They don't ask to be solved or implemented right away. Sometimes awareness needs time to settle before it turns into movement.

For now, carrying them gently is enough.

Today, notice one truth that's been revealed to you. Let yourself hold it without urgency. Trust that it will tell you what to do when the time is right.

August 10th: The Courage to Slow Down

Slowing down can take courage, especially in a culture that rewards constant motion, efficiency, and visible effort. Choosing slowness can feel like going against the grain, even when your body is clearly asking for it.

You may notice resistance when you rest. Old voices may question your worth. Familiar guilt can surface when you choose ease instead of productivity. These responses are learned, not true. They come from times when slowing down didn't feel safe.

But slowness has its own intelligence. It reminds you that not everything is meant to be rushed or optimized. That some experiences ask to be lived deliberately, not efficiently. That moving slower is sometimes the most honest response available to you.

Slowness allows integration. It gives your nervous system time to catch up. It lets experience become wisdom instead of just memory.

Today, practice slowing down, even if it feels uncomfortable. Pause longer than you normally would. Do one thing at a gentler pace. Trust the intelligence in that choice.

August 11th: Feeling the Weight You Carry

There are moments when the fullness of your life settles into your body. Not as overwhelm, but as weight. The joy you've known. The grief you've carried. The recovery. The hard choices. The moments you stayed when leaving would have been easier.

This weight isn't crushing. It's grounding. It gives you substance. It reminds you that your life has depth, that you have lived fully enough to be shaped by experience. You're not floating through your days untouched. You are rooted in what you've felt.

You don't need to lighten this weight or rush to set it down. You don't need to make it inspirational or turn it into a lesson. You can let it anchor you.

Today, acknowledge the weight of what you've lived. Feel it in your body. Let it remind you of your strength, your resilience, and your capacity to carry what matters.

August 12th: Letting Go of the Need to Maximize

There is a quiet invitation to stop trying to make the most of everything. To stop squeezing experiences for meaning, productivity, or proof that you're doing it right. Life doesn't ask to be optimized. It asks to be lived.

Something shifts when you release the urge to extract something from every moment. When pleasure is allowed to be simple. When enjoyment doesn't have to lead anywhere. When a day can pass without becoming a story, a milestone, or evidence of growth.

The impulse to maximize often comes from fear. Fear that time is slipping away. Fear that if you don't capture it, it won't count. But living fully doesn't require constant effort. Presence is already enough.

You don't need to turn experience into something more in order for it to matter. Being here is sufficient.

Today, release the need to maximize. Let one moment stand on its own, unmeasured and unenhanced. Trust that living it is enough.

August 13th: Trusting What's Sustainable

Over time, something becomes clearer. You begin to notice which rhythms you can live inside without strain and which ones quietly deplete you. The difference is felt in your body before it's understood in your mind.

Sustainability isn't about doing less for the sake of restraint. It's about care. About choosing ways of moving through your days that allow you to stay present without burning out. About honoring what you can return to again and again without losing yourself.

You're learning that not everything that's possible is worth pursuing. And not everything that looks impressive is livable. What lasts tends to be quieter. Steadier. More honest.

This awareness doesn't close your life down. It opens it in a different way. One that leaves room for breath.

Today, notice one choice that supports sustainability. Let yourself honor it, even if it means letting something else go.

August 14th: Standing Fully in Who You Are

There is a sense of fullness that doesn't need explanation. A way of being more settled inside yourself. Less reactive. More willing to let things unfold without needing to manage every outcome.

This doesn't mean everything is resolved. Questions still exist. Tender places still surface. But you are no longer at war with yourself. You don't rush to fix what arises. You meet it with more steadiness than before.

Standing in this fullness isn't about confidence or certainty. It's about self-acceptance. About allowing yourself to take up space in your own life without apology or justification.

You're not waiting to become someone else. You're here.

Today, stand in who you are. Let yourself feel the steadiness of that truth without needing to improve it.

August 15th: When the Light Changes

There comes a day when you notice the light is different. Still bright. Still warm. But softer at the edges. The sun lowers earlier. Shadows stretch longer across the ground. The quality of the day shifts, even though nothing has officially ended.

This noticing can stir emotion you weren't expecting. Gratitude mixed with sadness. Contentment brushing up against grief. You realize how deeply you've been living inside this season without stopping to name it.

Nothing has been lost. And yet, something is already changing.

This part of the season teaches you how to hold beauty without clinging. How to stay present without trying to preserve what was never meant to stay exactly the same.

Today, notice the quality of the light around you. Let it mirror what's shifting inside. Allow both appreciation and tenderness to coexist.

August 16th: Letting the Fullness Be Enough

There can be a quiet urge to squeeze more out of what's here. To do more. To experience everything. To make sure nothing is missed.

But fullness doesn't require completion. You don't need to exhaust yourself trying to capture it all. Some experiences are meant to be lived, not collected.

Sometimes fullness is already present. In your body. In your relationships. In the rhythm of your days. In the way you've learned to listen, rest, and respond with more honesty than before.

Letting this be enough is an act of trust. Trust that you haven't missed anything essential. Trust that what matters stays with you.

Today, allow the fullness of this moment to be sufficient. Don't add to it. Don't rush it. Let it be complete as it is.

August 17th: When You Feel Yourself Letting Go

Letting go rarely arrives as a single decision. It doesn't announce itself or ask to be witnessed. More often, it comes quietly, through small releases you might barely notice at first. A plan you don't make. An expectation you loosen. A role you step out of without explaining why.

These shifts don't come with drama. You don't mark them or defend them. You simply stop holding as tightly. Something inside you recognizes that the effort it once took to maintain certain things is no longer worth the cost.

This kind of letting go is gentle. It doesn't require force. It happens when something has run its course. When your body and your inner knowing agree that it's time.

Nothing here needs to be rushed. Nothing needs to be justified. Release unfolds in its own way, at its own pace.

Today, notice one small way you are already letting go. Let it happen without commentary. Trust that release doesn't need explanation to be real.

August 18th: Carrying Warmth Forward

Even as the season begins to turn, warmth lingers. It stays in the evenings that stretch just a little longer. In muscles that still remember long days outside. In the way your body relaxes more easily than it once did.

This warmth doesn't disappear when the days begin to change. It moves inward. It becomes something you carry rather than something you depend on. It shows up in how you treat yourself with more patience. In how you pace your life with less urgency. In the softness you allow instead of pushing through.

Warmth becomes internal now. A way of being rather than a condition of the weather.

You don't lose what this season gave you. You integrate it. You carry it quietly into whatever comes next.

Today, notice where warmth lives inside you. In your chest. In your breath. In the way you respond to yourself. Let it stay. Let it become part of you.

August 19th: Trusting What Has Settled

Not everything needs to be revisited. Not every insight needs to be reworked or examined again. Some lessons have already done their work. They've settled into your bones, shaping how you move through the world without needing your constant attention.

You may notice this in subtle ways. You react less quickly. You explain yourself less. You allow silence to exist without rushing to fill it. You trust your instincts without needing to debate them.

This isn't disengagement. It's integration. It's what happens when something has been learned deeply enough that it no longer needs rehearsal.

Trusting what has settled is an act of confidence. It says, I don't need to keep proving this to myself.

Today, trust one thing that feels settled. Let it stand without revisiting it. Allow yourself to move forward without reopening what no longer needs tending.

August 20th: The Quiet Readiness

There is a readiness that doesn't rush you. It doesn't demand clarity or immediate action. It doesn't arrive with plans or answers.

It feels more like a quiet knowing. A sense that something new will come when it's time. That you'll recognize it when it does. That you don't need to search or force anything into place.

This readiness is patient. It trusts timing. It understands that preparation doesn't always look like effort. Sometimes it looks like rest. Sometimes it looks like waiting without anxiety.

Nothing here needs to be pushed. Nothing is lost by allowing things to unfold naturally. What's meant to take shape will do so when the conditions are right.

Today, notice the quiet readiness within you. Don't define it. Don't rush it into form. Let it remain open, trusting that it knows what it's doing.

August 21st: Living the In-Between

You are no longer where you were, and you are not yet somewhere else. You are in between. Past one chapter. Not yet inside the next.

This space can feel unfamiliar if you're used to clear direction or resolution. It may bring uncertainty, restlessness, or the urge to hurry yourself forward. But it can also hold something else. Room. Breath. Possibility without pressure.

The in-between doesn't ask you to decide. It asks you to stay. To live inside the pause without demanding that it become something more.

There is value here. Things quietly reorganize themselves in this space. Insight forms without being chased. Clarity takes shape without force.

Today, allow yourself to live fully in the in-between. Don't rush it. Don't treat it as unfinished. Let this space be exactly what it is.

August 22nd: When the Air Feels Different

There is a morning when you step outside and the air surprises you. Still warm. Still familiar. But touched with something else. A thin edge of coolness. A hint of what's coming.

It's subtle enough that you might miss it if you're distracted. But your body notices. You breathe a little deeper. You pause for half a second longer. Something registers before you have words for it.

Change often arrives this way. Quietly. Without announcement. It doesn't demand that you respond or prepare. It simply asks to be felt.

This kind of noticing doesn't require action. It invites awareness.

Today, notice how the air feels against your skin. Let your body take it in. Let it tell you what it's ready to say, without asking it to explain itself.

August 23rd: Letting Nostalgia Pass Through

This part of the season has a way of stirring memory without warning. The smell of cut grass. The hum of insects at dusk. Light slanting through trees at just the right angle. Small sensory moments open doors you didn't intend to walk through.

A swell of feeling rises. A remembering. A longing. A sadness that doesn't quite have a story attached to it. You may feel it in your chest before you understand it in your mind.

You don't need to push this away or analyze it. Nostalgia doesn't mean you want to go backward. It means you've lived something that mattered. It means your life has texture. Depth. History.

These feelings don't ask to be fixed. They ask to be felt and released.

Today, allow a memory to pass through you. Don't cling to it. Don't resist it. Let it move the way it needs to.

August 24th: Letting the Moment Be Enough

There can be an urge to hold tighter. To plan more. To document. To make sure nothing slips away unnoticed. Grasping can feel like protection, but it often pulls you out of the moment you're trying to preserve.

Presence asks for something different. It invites you to stay with what's here without reaching ahead or pulling back. To allow a moment to exist without asking it to last longer than it will.

You don't lose what matters by letting it move. You honor it by being fully inside it while it's here.

There is respect in allowing experiences to pass naturally.

Today, choose presence in one moment. Stay without grasping. Let the experience be complete without trying to keep it.

August 25th: Trusting What You've Absorbed

You don't need to remember every lesson life has offered. You don't need to summarize, extract, or make meaning out of everything you've lived.

Much of what you've learned has already moved beneath language. It lives in how you respond instead of react. In how you rest without guilt. In what you no longer tolerate. In what you instinctively protect.

This is wisdom absorbed, not studied. Integration rather than insight.

You don't need to hold it consciously for it to guide you.

Today, trust that what you needed has already taken root. Let yourself move forward without carrying every explanation with you.

August 26th: When You Stop Preparing for Loss

There is a habit many of us carry quietly. Bracing for the end of good things before they happen. Preparing for disappointment. Softening joy in advance so it won't hurt as much later.

This habit often comes from experience. From knowing how quickly things can change. But it keeps you partially absent from moments that deserve your full attention.

There is another way of being. Letting beauty exist without anticipating its loss. Letting joy arrive without bargaining with it or holding it at arm's length.

Nothing lasts forever. But that doesn't mean you need to leave before it's over.

Today, allow yourself to enjoy something fully. Don't prepare for its ending. Let it be whole while it's here.

August 27th: Carrying Gratitude Without Clinging

Gratitude can take on a quieter shape. Not loud or outward, but something that settles gently and lingers.

It's possible to appreciate what has been given without needing to keep it exactly as it is. To say thank you without reaching for more. To notice abundance without trying to possess it.

You may notice how different this feels from the kind of gratitude that carries a hint of fear – the quiet worry that what you love could be taken away.

This kind of gratitude doesn't require holding on tightly or freezing time. It leaves room for appreciation without attachment.

Gratitude begins to feel less like a reaction and more like a way of moving through the world.

Today, name one thing you're grateful for. Let it be complete on its own, without adding anything to it.

August 28th: Standing Gently at the Threshold

There is a moment when you realize you are no longer fully inside what was, but not yet living what comes next. It doesn't feel like loss, and it doesn't feel like arrival. It feels like standing at the edge of something that's changing.

You don't have to cross yet. There is permission to pause here. To look back with tenderness, without rewriting the past. To look ahead with curiosity, without rushing toward answers or certainty.

Thresholds are spaces of transition. They hold both memory and possibility. They ask for presence rather than decision, and respect rather than speed.

Nothing here needs to be resolved. Nothing needs to be forced into clarity. What's forming will take shape in its own time.

Today, allow yourself to stand gently at the threshold. Feel the ground beneath you. Trust your own sense of timing. You will step forward when you're ready – and not a moment before.

August 29th: Letting Experience Speak for Itself

There comes a point when you stop trying to name everything you've lived. You no longer need to label it good or hard or transformative.

You simply know it.

What you've moved through has settled in your body. In your energy. In the way you've slowed without resistance. In the way you've listened without urgency. It has shaped you quietly, without asking to be analyzed or explained.

You don't need to turn it into a story or extract a lesson for it to matter.

Some experiences are meant to be felt, not translated.

Today, let what you've lived speak for itself. Resist the urge to explain it. Let knowing be enough.

August 30th: When Something Has Quietly Shifted

Sometimes change doesn't arrive with a decision or a declaration. It shows up in small ways. In how you no longer feel the need to explain yourself. In how certain things don't pull at you the way they once did. In how you let something pass without trying to hold it in place.

There is a kind of readiness that doesn't ask for attention. A quiet sense that something has settled into you and no longer needs managing.

What once required effort now feels natural. What once felt essential feels complete.

Today, notice one place where you're no longer gripping the way you used to. Let that be enough evidence that something has already shifted.

August 31st: What Was Always There

Every summer for years, I returned to the same place. The lake. The shoreline. The familiar rhythms of being there. And each time, I knew the causeway existed – a long stretch reaching across the water – but I never went out onto it. I noticed it without entering it. It stayed just outside my experience.

Until one year, it didn't.

I stepped onto it for the first time and felt how much I had missed. The openness. The steady expanse of water on both sides. The way time slowed without effort. A walk with the dog. A jog. A long, unhurried pass where nothing was required except attention. The causeway hadn't changed. I had.

Now I look forward to it every year. I make space for it. I let it hold me in different ways – moving, resting, taking it all in. What surprises me most is not that it's beautiful, but that it was always offering this, even when I wasn't ready to receive it.

There are many things like this in a life. Places. Moments. Quiet invitations we live alongside for years before we finally say yes. Beauty and meaning that don't call out, but wait.

Today, notice something you've been living near but not fully inside. Let yourself slow enough to enter it. Receive what's been there all along.

September

♡

A season of noticing what no longer needs to be held.

September 1st: The Feeling of Beginning Again

There is a beginning here that doesn't announce itself loudly. It arrives quietly, through a shift in light, a coolness in the air that wakes you up without startling you. Mornings feel more intentional. Evenings invite earlier rest. Something in you senses a return to rhythm without the pressure to reinvent your life.

This kind of beginning feels different from the ones that demand declarations or resolutions. It doesn't ask you to become someone new. It asks you to remember who you already are beneath the noise, beneath the striving.

You've lived enough to know that you don't need a clean slate to start again. You don't need to erase what came before. What you need is presence. Attention. A willingness to step forward without abandoning yourself.

Beginnings like this are subtle. They don't require bold moves or dramatic change. They ask for alignment.

Today, notice what feels like a natural beginning in your life right now. Step into it gently, without forcing momentum. Let it unfold at its own pace.

September 2nd: When the Body Wakes Up

There is a clarity the body recognizes before the mind does. A sense of readiness that arrives quietly. Breath deepens. Movement feels more available. You may notice a desire to orient yourself again, to engage with the day in a way that feels intentional rather than reactive.

This isn't urgency. It's responsiveness. A calm readiness that comes from feeling supported rather than depleted.

Your body is recalibrating. Re-entering a rhythm that feels steadier and more sustainable. You might find yourself wanting to move a little more, stretch a little deeper, or create order where things once felt scattered.

This is your body remembering what balance feels like.

Today, listen closely for what your body is ready for. Follow that cue with care, not obligation. Let movement come from readiness, not pressure.

September 3rd: Letting Structure Support You

Sometimes a gentle rhythm begins to take shape. The day feels easier to move through. Time feels less scattered. Small routines settle in without much effort.

Structure can feel different than it once did. Less like something you use to manage yourself, more like something that quietly supports you. A way of holding your energy instead of asking more from it.

You may notice how comforting it feels to have parts of your day already decided. Not as rules, but as anchors. Something steady to return to when everything else feels open and undefined.

In this way, structure doesn't limit freedom. It gives it something stable to move around.

Today, notice one part of your day that provides this quiet steadiness. Spend a moment there.

September 4th: The Relief of Honesty

There are moments when things come into focus. The noise quiets. What matters feels clearer. There's less impulse to hide or hedge, internally or externally.

You may feel drawn toward honesty then. Not the kind that needs to be dramatic or confessional, but the quiet kind that's steady and true. Honesty with yourself about what you want. What you don't. Where you're willing to show up and where you're not anymore.

This honesty can feel relieving. Like setting something down you've been carrying unnecessarily. Like allowing your words and actions to finally match what you've known inside.

You don't need to justify this clarity. You don't need to soften it to make it easier for others to receive.

Today, practice one small act of honesty. Say what's true without over-explaining. Notice how that truth settles in your body once it's spoken.

September 5th: When You Feel More Grounded

Groundedness isn't something you force or chase. It arrives when your body feels safe enough to settle. When your nervous system no longer needs to stay alert or braced.

You may notice it in small ways. Moving through the day with less urgency. Thoughts that don't scatter as easily. A clearer sense of where you are, instead of constantly reaching for what's next.

This steadiness didn't appear overnight. It formed through listening. Through responding. Through choosing presence again and again, even when it felt unfamiliar.

There is a quiet confidence here. A sense of being where your feet are, both literally and emotionally.

Today, notice one moment where you feel grounded. Stay with it a little longer. Let your body recognize the safety of being fully here.

September 6th: Full Circle

Some friendships begin so early they feel woven into your life. You grow up alongside each other, sharing childhood years before you fully understand what friendship even means. Over time, life pulls you in different directions. You stay in touch here and there, checking in from a distance as each of you builds a life of your own.

Then, sometimes, those friendships find their way back. Not loudly or all at once, but naturally. When they do, there is an immediate sense of familiarity, as if no time has passed. The connection feels steady, grounded, and surprisingly deep.

You realize that this person has always mattered. That they know you in a way that doesn't require explanation. The bond may look different now, shaped by growth and experience, but its foundation remains unchanged.

Some people are not meant to stay close through every season. They return when the time is right, reminding you that certain connections are meant to last, even when they take the long way around.

Today, notice the friendships that have come back into your life. Honor the quiet joy of recognizing someone who has always belonged there.

September 7th: Standing in Clearer Light

The light is different now. It doesn't blur or soften edges the way it once did. It clarifies. It reveals what's been there all along, quietly waiting to be seen.

This kind of light can feel exposing. You notice what matters more clearly. You see what no longer fits. What drains you. What feels sustainable and what doesn't. There's less room for illusion, but also less need for it.

Clarity can be relieving. You don't have to guess as much anymore. You don't have to convince yourself. Things simply show themselves.

This awareness doesn't demand action or urgency. It asks for honesty. For seeing without rushing to fix or change.

Today, stand in this clearer light. Notice what becomes obvious when you stop looking away. Trust what you see, even if you're not ready to act on it yet.

September 8th: Staying Curious

Sometimes interest appears before confidence.
You notice a pull toward something new – a class, a skill, a way of moving your body, a subject you don't yet understand.
There's no plan attached to it. Just curiosity.

You might also notice the old voice that follows.
The one that wonders if it's too late.
If you should already know more by now.
If beginners are supposed to be younger, faster, or more certain.

But curiosity doesn't belong to a particular age or stage.
It belongs to being here.

Learning doesn't always mean starting from scratch. Sometimes it means letting yourself be new again – open, unpolished, interested without needing to be impressive.

You don't have to commit.
You don't have to explain the interest.
You don't even have to be good at it.

Today, notice one thing you're curious about but haven't allowed yourself to explore. Let the interest exist without deciding what it needs to become.

September 9th: Choosing What Gets Your Energy

Over time, something shifts.
What once felt manageable begins to feel draining. What you used to push through asks for reconsideration. At the same time, certain things start to feel more essential than ever.

This isn't selfishness. It's clarity. You're no longer giving your energy away automatically or out of habit. You understand its value now. You know how quickly it can be depleted when it's spent in places that don't return care.

Energy spent wisely feels different in the body. Lighter. Cleaner. More sustainable. There's less resentment, less recovery needed afterward.

You don't need to explain these choices. You don't need permission to protect what sustains you.

Today, notice where your energy goes. Choose one place to spend it more intentionally. Let that choice reflect respect for yourself and the life you're building.

September 10th: The Quiet Strength of Boundaries

Boundaries feel more natural now. Less like a decision you debate and more like a response you trust. There's no drama in it. Just awareness.

You're no longer setting boundaries to prove something or protect yourself from imagined harm. You're setting them because you know what helps you stay steady. You know where you end and where others begin.

There is relief in this clarity. In not needing to explain every choice. In allowing yourself to say no without rehearsing. In choosing what supports you without apology.

Boundaries don't harden you. They allow you to remain open without losing yourself in the process.

Today, honor one boundary that helps you feel protected and steady. Let it be simple. Let it be enough.

September 11th: Letting Yourself Be Clear

Seeing clearly can feel surprisingly vulnerable. When things come into focus, there is less room to hide from what you know. Fewer places to tuck away discomfort. Less ability to tell yourself stories that keep you comfortable but stuck.

You may notice the instinct to soften the truth. To delay a decision. To stay in the familiar a little longer, even when you know it no longer fits. Not because you're avoiding growth, but because clarity asks something real of you.

But clarity isn't here to rush you or demand immediate action. It doesn't shout. It doesn't pressure. It simply illuminates what's already true and waits for you to meet it when you're ready.

Seeing clearly allows you to move forward with honesty instead of confusion. It reduces the quiet friction that comes from pretending you don't know what you know.

Today, notice one truth that feels clear. Let it stand without minimizing it, negotiating with it, or rushing past it. Allow clarity to be a guide, not a threat.

September 12th: Trusting Yourself Over the Noise

At some point, the noise quiets just enough for you to hear yourself again beneath the constant input.

You may notice how little you reach for outside reassurance now. Fewer opinions. Less checking. Less need to crowd-source your decisions or explain them before you've even made them.

This trust didn't appear overnight. It grew slowly through lived experience. Through moments when you listened inward and discovered you could handle what followed. Through self-honesty that taught you the difference between fear and intuition.

You know what feels right not because you're certain about everything, but because you're willing to listen.

Today, in one small moment, trust your own knowing over the surrounding noise. Let your inner voice be enough without needing backup.

September 13th: Carrying What Grounds You

Grounding becomes essential at certain points in life. Not as a rule or a discipline, but as a form of care. You naturally reach for what steadies you. Familiar rituals. Consistent movement. Quiet routines that bring you back into your body.

These aren't habits you force yourself to maintain. They're supports you choose because you've felt what happens when you lose touch with them. You know how disorienting it feels to drift too far from yourself.

Grounding doesn't control your life. It anchors it. It gives you something solid to return to when things feel uncertain or emotionally charged.

Today, return to one grounding practice. Let it anchor you without expectation. Let it remind your body that you are here, supported, and allowed to take up space.

September 14th: Standing Firm Without Hardening

There is a difference between being firm and becoming rigid. Between knowing where you stand and closing yourself off. This distinction becomes clearer now.

You can hold your values without gripping them. You can say no without hostility. You can remain open even while standing your ground. This balance doesn't come from theory. It's learned through living. Through trial and error. Through moments when you chose honesty over approval.

Being firm doesn't require armor. It requires clarity. It allows you to stay rooted without becoming brittle or defensive.

You are allowed to be steady and soft at the same time. Strength does not cancel tenderness.

Today, notice one place where you stand firm while remaining open. Let yourself trust that balance.

September 15th: When Responsibility Feels Different

There was a time when responsibility felt heavy in a way that flattened you. Obligations stacked up. Expectations pressed in. You carried more than was yours because you didn't know how to set it down.

Now, responsibility feels different. Not lighter, exactly, but clearer. You recognize what belongs to you and what doesn't. You choose what you're willing to hold instead of absorbing everything by default.

This kind of responsibility doesn't drain you. It steadies you. It feels intentional rather than imposed. You engage because you want to, not because you're afraid of what will happen if you don't.

You are no longer confusing responsibility with self-sacrifice.

Today, notice one responsibility you carry with intention rather than obligation. Let yourself feel the difference in your body.

September 16th: The Strength of Being Steady

There is a kind of strength that doesn't announce itself.
It doesn't need attention or approval. It simply shows up, again and again, clear in its values and consistent in its presence.

You know this strength when you feel it.
It's the person who says what they mean and means what they say. The one who follows through. The one who doesn't disappear when things get uncomfortable, but also doesn't overcomplicate what's true.

This steadiness isn't rigidity.
It's discernment. It's knowing where you stand and not needing to perform around it. It's reliability without resentment. Honesty without excess explanation.

In a world that often rewards loudness or constant flexibility, this kind of grounded presence is rare.
It builds trust quietly. It makes other people feel safe without trying to.

Today, honor the strength it takes to be steady. To be someone others can rely on – without losing yourself in the process. Let that kind of integrity matter.

September 17th: Learning to Loosen

Some people move through life with a lightness that can't be taught. They don't cling to what doesn't matter. They know what to carry and what to let pass. Being near them reminds you that not everything needs to be held so tightly.

Free spirits have a way of loosening your grip. They laugh more easily. They adapt. They trust the unfolding of things without needing to control the outcome. Their presence gently challenges the idea that responsibility has to feel heavy or that care requires constant effort.

From them, you learn that life holds more when you stop bracing against it. That joy has room to arrive when you're not managing every detail. That freedom isn't about abandoning what matters, but about releasing what doesn't.

There is wisdom in this kind of living. A quiet permission to breathe, to trust, to let things be simpler than you imagined they had to be.

Today, notice one place where you can loosen your grip. Let something that doesn't truly matter fall away, and see what lightness becomes possible when you do.

September 18th: When Grief Deepens

Grief doesn't always arrive loudly. It doesn't always come with tears or sharp longing. Sometimes it lives quietly in the body. In moments of pause. In the awareness of what once was and will not return.

At certain points, grief can deepen without becoming overwhelming. It settles into you – less dramatic, but more present. You may feel it as a sudden tenderness. In the way certain memories surface without warning. In a softness that wasn't there before.

This quieter grief isn't asking to be fixed or explained. It's asking to be acknowledged. To be given space without being rushed toward resolution.

This is not a setback. It's integration. A sign that loss has become part of you without consuming you.

Today, allow grief to exist gently. Notice where it lives in your body. Let it be felt without trying to make sense of it or move past it.

September 19th: No Longer Negotiating Your Worth

There was a time when your worth felt conditional. Dependent on productivity. Approval. How well you held everything together without asking for too much in return.

You may have learned to bargain with yourself. To earn rest. To justify your needs. To believe your value rose and fell with your output or your usefulness to others.

Now, something has shifted. You're less willing to negotiate what should never have been up for debate. Less inclined to prove yourself through effort or endurance.

Your worth does not fluctuate with your productivity. It does not disappear when you slow down. It does not need constant reinforcement to remain real.

Today, notice one moment where you stop negotiating your worth. Where you choose to stand in it quietly, without explanation. Let that steadiness be enough.

September 20th: Carrying Less Into the Next Season

As the equinox approaches, there is a natural invitation to lighten your load. Not dramatically. Not all at once. Gently.

You begin to notice what you don't want to carry forward. The tension that no longer serves you. The expectations that don't fit who you are now. The ways you've been holding yourself together out of habit rather than necessity.

Letting go doesn't require an announcement. It doesn't need justification. It begins with honesty. With acknowledging what feels heavy and allowing yourself to release it without guilt.

You are allowed to move into what comes next with less weight on your shoulders. With more space in your body. With fewer obligations that don't reflect your truth.

Today, choose one thing to release before the season changes. Let yourself step forward carrying less, trusting that you don't need it anymore.

September 21st: Standing at the Edge of Change

There is a particular stillness that arrives just before a shift. You can feel it if you pause long enough. In the air. In your body. In the subtle awareness that something is turning, even if you can't yet name what comes next.

This moment doesn't ask you to act. It doesn't require decisions or declarations. It invites you to stand here, at the edge, and notice what has brought you to this point. The growth. The losses. The adjustments you've made quietly along the way.

You don't need to rush into what's next. You're allowed to linger. To honor what has been without clinging to it. To acknowledge what you've learned without needing to summarize it.

Change does not erase you. It doesn't demand that you become someone new overnight. It meets you exactly where you are, carrying everything you already know how to be.

Today, stand at the edge of change. Feel your feet on the ground. Trust your readiness, even if it feels calm rather than excited.

September 22nd: When Light and Dark Meet

The equinox arrives without announcement. No fanfare. Just a quiet balance that reveals itself if you're paying attention.

Light and dark share the sky equally today. Neither tries to dominate. Neither apologizes for existing. They simply coexist, each holding its place.

There is something deeply reassuring in this. A reminder that your life does not need to be all light to be whole. That the darker seasons you've moved through were not mistakes or detours. That rest, grief, joy, effort, and stillness all belong to the same story.

You may feel steadier today without knowing why. Or you may feel tender, aware of how much you've carried to arrive here. Both responses make sense. Both are welcome.

Balance doesn't mean everything feels easy or resolved. It means nothing needs to be denied in order for you to be whole.

Today, honor both the light and the shadow within you. Let them exist side by side without trying to fix, justify, or prioritize one over the other.

September 23rd: When Love Keeps Pace

Love is not about moving in perfect unison. It's about choosing to keep pace, even when your steps are uneven. Even when one of you is tired, distracted, or moving through something the other cannot fully see.

There are seasons when you feel perfectly aligned – laughter easy, connection effortless. And there are seasons when love looks quieter. Slower. More deliberate. When staying requires intention rather than momentum.

Real love makes room for this. It doesn't demand perfect alignment. It allows each person to grow, to change, to stumble, knowing the promise is not to stay ahead or behind, but to stay near.

Sometimes love sounds like patience. Sometimes it sounds like forgiveness. Sometimes it sounds like, *I'm here. I'm not going anywhere. We'll figure this out together.*

This kind of love holds more than one truth at once. Strength and vulnerability. Joy and strain. Certainty and doubt. It doesn't ask you to resolve the tension. It asks you to keep choosing each other inside it.

Today, reflect on a love that has kept pace with you. Let yourself feel the steadiness of being met, again and again, even as you both continue to change.

September 24th: The Gentle Pull Inward

At certain points, something inside you begins to respond instinctively. You crave quieter evenings. Softer mornings. Fewer demands on your attention. More space to think, feel, and breathe without interruption.

This inward pull is not avoidance. It's not withdrawal. It's wisdom. Your system recognizes when it's time to turn toward reflection rather than expansion.

You may feel drawn to slower rituals. To silence. To moments where you don't need to perform or produce anything. This isn't a loss of ambition. It's a different kind of listening.

You don't need to justify this turning inward. You're allowed to follow it without explanation.

Today, give yourself permission to turn inward, even briefly. Sit with yourself without distraction. Notice what wants to be heard when the noise softens.

September 25th: What Has Taken Root

Not everything from this year will stay with you. Some experiences were meant to pass through. Some lessons did their work and moved on without asking to be remembered.

But some changes have taken root. They are no longer fragile or experimental. They don't require effort to maintain. They live in your responses now. In your boundaries. In how you speak to yourself when no one else is listening.

These roots were formed slowly. Through repetition. Through choice. Through moments when you stayed instead of leaving, listened instead of overriding, softened instead of bracing.

You don't need to question what has settled. You don't need proof that it's real.

Today, notice one way you are different now. Feel it in your body, not your thoughts. Trust that what has taken root will continue to grow, even without your constant attention.

September 26th: The Strength of Showing Up Again

There is a quiet courage in showing up again and again. Not in dramatic ways. Not with big declarations or visible breakthroughs. But in ordinary, almost invisible ones.

You wake up. You tend to what's needed. You take care of what you can and rest when you're able. You keep choosing care over collapse, even when no one is watching. Even when it feels repetitive. Even when it feels unremarkable.

This kind of strength rarely gets recognized. It doesn't draw attention. But it builds lives that last. It creates stability where chaos once lived. It lays foundations that can actually hold weight.

Life understands that rhythm. Deep roots. Slow growth. Daily tending. Nothing rushed. Nothing wasted.

Today, honor one small way you continue to show up for yourself. Let it matter, even if it feels ordinary.

September 27th: When You Stop Overexplaining

At some point, you realize you're tired of explaining yourself. Not out of defensiveness or withdrawal, but out of trust. You know why you've chosen what you've chosen. You've lived the consequences. You've listened carefully.

You no longer need every decision to be understood in order for it to be valid. You don't feel compelled to soften, justify, or translate yourself before you act. You let your choices stand where they are.

This isn't hardness. It's confidence that has grown quietly over time. Confidence shaped by experience, not approval. Confidence that doesn't need witnesses.

Letting go of overexplaining creates space. Space to move freely. Space to respond honestly instead of defensively. Space to live without narrating every step.

Today, allow one choice to exist without explanation. Notice how it feels to trust yourself enough to let it stand.

September 28th: Feeling Supported by Your Life

There are moments when you move through your day and notice how much is already holding you. Familiar spaces. Well-worn paths. Small routines that carry you without much thought.

An ordinary moment can feel steady in a way that's hard to explain. Not exciting. Not dramatic. Just quietly supportive.

You may sense how your life, as it is right now, meets you in ways you once had to work for. How the effort you've poured in over time has softened into something that now holds you back.

Nothing needs to be named in these moments. Nothing needs to be shared. It's simply a feeling of being supported by what surrounds you.

Today, notice one place where your life feels this way.

September 29th: Preparing With Care, Not Fear

Preparation doesn't have to come from anxiety. It doesn't need to be driven by worry or anticipation of loss. It can come from attentiveness instead.

You begin to adjust naturally. Pulling out warmer layers. Shifting routines. Creating space for rest and reflection. These changes don't feel frantic. They feel responsive.

There's no panic here. Just readiness. A trust in your ability to meet what's coming because you've learned how to listen to yourself along the way.

Care-based preparation is gentle. It respects your limits. It doesn't demand urgency or perfection.

Today, prepare for what's ahead with care rather than fear. Let readiness feel calm instead of tense.

September 30th: Carrying Yourself Differently

Every now and then, you catch a glimpse of yourself in a quiet moment and realize something has softened.

Not in what you're doing, but in how you're being. A gentler response where there once was tension. A steadiness in places that used to feel charged. A kinder voice meeting you where criticism once lived.

Nothing announces this change. It appears in ordinary moments. In the way you move through a conversation. In how you return to yourself after being pulled outward. In the absence of reactions you once knew well.

There's a tenderness in recognizing this. A sense of care you now carry with you without trying.

Today, notice one small way you meet yourself differently than you once did.

October

♡

Letting go of what no longer serves, rooted in what remains.

October 1st: When the Air Changes Everything

You notice it the moment you step outside. The air feels sharper, cooler, more awake. Breathing takes on a different quality, as if your lungs are finally clearing after months of warmth and softness. Each inhale feels more deliberate. Each exhale more complete.

This shift does something to your attention. You're not lulled by ease or distracted by abundance anymore. You arrive more fully in your body. More present. More aware of what's real and what's been quietly waiting to be felt.

This season acts like a truth teller. It doesn't rush you forward or offer distraction. It asks you to notice. To feel how your body responds when the environment changes and there's no hiding from it. The world looks familiar, but your experience of it is different now. More grounded. More honest.

This change can feel grounding and unsettling at the same time. It brings clarity without demanding answers. Awareness without urgency.

Today, take a slow breath outside. Let the air wake you up. Let it bring you fully into where you are, without asking you to be anywhere else.

October 2nd: The Way Memory Lives in the Body

This time of year has a way of unlocking memory without warning. The smell of damp leaves. The sound of wind moving through branches. The early darkness arriving before you're ready. These sensations slip past logic and land directly in the body.

You may feel it as a tightening in your chest. A softness behind the eyes. A familiar ache or warmth that doesn't come with a clear story attached. Memory doesn't always arrive with images or words. Often, it arrives as sensation.

This remembering isn't here to overwhelm you. It's here to remind you that you have lived. That your life has texture and depth. That what shaped you still matters, even if it no longer defines you.

You don't need to analyze these moments or trace them back to their origin. You don't need to explain why they arrive when they do.

Today, notice where memory shows up in your body. Let it be felt without interpretation. Allow your body to remember without asking it to make sense.

October 3rd: When Grief Feels Close but Gentle

Grief doesn't always arrive loudly. It doesn't always come with tears or sharp longing. Sometimes it lives quietly in the body. In moments of pause. In the awareness of what once was and will not return.

You may find your thoughts drifting toward people you've lost. Versions of yourself that no longer exist. Seasons of life that ended without ceremony or closure. The remembering feels softer now, but no less real.

This kind of grief doesn't mean you're moving backward. It means you've integrated enough to feel what once had to be buried just to survive. You have more capacity now. More room.

Grief isn't asking to be solved or reframed. It's asking to be honored. To be allowed a seat beside you instead of being pushed away.

Today, allow grief to sit near you. Notice how it feels when you don't try to outrun it. Let its presence be quiet, and let that be enough.

October 4th: Doing One Thing With Care

Not every day asks for insight.
Not every moment needs to be examined.

Some days simply ask you to do one small thing with care.

To fold the blanket slowly instead of tossing it aside.
To rinse the mug instead of leaving it in the sink.
To water the plant you keep meaning to get to.
To answer one message you've been avoiding.

These are not chores.
They are ways of placing yourself back into your life.

Care is a form of presence.
Action, when it's gentle, can steady you more than reflection ever could.

You don't have to understand how you feel in order to move your hands with intention.
You don't have to solve anything to tend to what's in front of you.

Today, choose one small thing and do it with care. Let that be enough.

October 5th: The Relief of Being Honest

There is a particular relief that comes with admitting when you're not okay. With letting go of the performance of being fine. With no longer needing to minimize or smooth over your experience.

You may notice how honesty changes the way you breathe. The way your body settles when you stop holding yourself together for appearance's sake. When you allow what's real to take up space.

You don't need to pretend strength. You don't need to package your feelings into something more acceptable. Honesty doesn't make you weaker. It makes you lighter.

You are allowed to show up exactly as you are, without apology or explanation.

Today, tell yourself the truth about how you're really doing. Let that honesty soften you instead of hardening you. Let it be a form of care.

October 6th: What Letting Go Really Looks Like

Letting go is rarely dramatic. It doesn't usually arrive with clarity or ceremony. More often, it happens quietly. In the moment you stop fighting something that has already changed. In the breath you release when you realize you don't have to carry this anymore.

This season shows you how to let go without force. Leaves fall without resistance. Not because they failed. Not because they weren't needed. But because their work is complete. Their letting go is not rejection. It's fulfillment.

You may be holding onto something that once kept you safe. A role. A belief. A way of being that mattered deeply at one point in your life. Letting go of it now does not erase its importance. It honors the purpose it served and acknowledges that you've grown beyond it.

Release doesn't need to be abrupt. It can be gentle. It can happen one breath at a time.

Today, notice one thing you're ready to loosen your grip on. Let yourself soften around it. Allow it to fall without forcing the moment.

October 7th: Standing Steady in Change

Change rarely arrives all at once. It moves gradually, reshaping your routines, your attention, your inner landscape.

You may feel this shift inside yourself. A longing for more quiet. More grounding. Less noise and stimulation. A desire to simplify instead of stretch.

There's no need to brace against this movement. You don't have to resist it or rush to understand it. You can remain steady and let change move through you.

Steadiness isn't rigidity. It's trust. Trust that you can stay rooted even as things evolve. Trust that change doesn't require you to lose yourself.

Today, ground yourself in one steady practice. Something familiar. Something supportive. Let it hold you as things continue to shift.

October 8th: When You Stop Running From Yourself

There are times when staying busy feels like survival. When movement, noise, and distraction help you avoid what feels too big to sit with.

Eventually, those exits quiet down. The pace slows just enough for you to notice what rises when you stop running. Thoughts you've postponed. Feelings you've sidestepped. Needs you didn't have room for before.

At first, this can feel uncomfortable. Even unsettling. But there is relief here too. You're no longer scattering your energy to avoid yourself. You're learning how to stay.

This staying doesn't require courage or confidence. It requires presence. A willingness to remain with yourself as you are, without needing to change anything first.

Today, notice one moment when you stop running. When you remain right where you are. Let yourself experience the quiet strength of staying.

October 9th: The Tender Work of Self-Compassion

Self-compassion is often mistaken for weakness or indulgence. But real self-compassion is sturdy. It doesn't disappear when things feel unresolved or uncomfortable. It stays.

This season may surface old patterns. Regrets you thought you'd made peace with. Familiar self-criticism. Stories about who you should have been or how things should have turned out.

This isn't failure. It's an invitation.

Instead of tightening against yourself, you soften. Instead of pushing forward, you pause. You speak to yourself with the same care you would offer someone you love who is hurting or unsure.

Self-compassion doesn't excuse harm. It creates the safety needed for healing.

Today, practice one moment of self-compassion. Let it interrupt an old habit of harshness. Notice how your body responds when you choose gentleness instead.

October 10th: When Forgiveness Begins Inside

Forgiveness is often framed as something you offer others. But the deeper work begins within you.

You may still carry resentment toward yourself. For what you didn't know. For what you couldn't change. For the ways you coped when you were doing your best to survive. These places often surface now, not to punish you, but to ask for care.

Forgiveness doesn't rewrite the past. It doesn't pretend things didn't hurt. It loosens the grip those moments still have on you.

You don't need to rush this process. You don't need to reach resolution. Even willingness is enough. Even curiosity is enough.

Today, notice one place where forgiveness could begin inside you. Let it unfold gently, without expectation. Let the first movement be kindness.

October 11th: Sitting With What You Avoided

There are truths you once learned to step around. Feelings that felt too big to touch safely. Conversations you never finished having, even with yourself.

Avoidance was not a failure. It was protection. It helped you survive what you didn't yet have the capacity to face.

Now, those places may rise gently, without force. Not all at once. Not demanding resolution. They surface because something in you knows you are steadier now than you once were.

You don't need to shame what you avoided. It served a purpose. But you also don't need to live around it anymore.

Today, sit briefly with one thing you once avoided. Notice it without judgment. Remind yourself that you are here now, and that you are safe to feel what once felt impossible.

October 12th: The Strength of Letting Yourself Feel

Feeling deeply does not weaken you. It expands your capacity to live honestly. Sometimes you learn this by watching someone you love feel everything so openly, so honestly, without trying to hide it.

There may have been a time when emotions felt dangerous. Something to control, contain, or move past quickly. But this season reminds you that emotions are movement. Energy passing through, not something meant to be trapped inside you.

You may have seen this in someone close to you – how learning to feel safely changed the way they move through the world.

You can feel sadness without drowning in it. Anger without exploding. Grief without collapsing. You can stay connected to yourself even as feelings rise and fall.

This is not something you force. It's something you allow. Trusting that your body knows how to move through what it feels when you don't interrupt the process.

Today, allow one feeling to move through you without resistance. Stay present with it. Notice how it changes when you let it flow instead of pushing it away.

October 13th: When You Choose Gentleness

Gentleness is a choice. Especially when you are tired. Especially when old patterns resurface and the familiar urge to push harder or demand more shows up.

You may notice a reflex toward criticism. Toward tightening. Toward telling yourself to do better, be stronger, try harder. These responses often come from fear, not truth.

Gentleness offers another way. It keeps you connected to yourself instead of turning against yourself. It allows growth without harm.

Choosing gentleness does not mean lowering standards or avoiding responsibility. It means recognizing that care creates more sustainable change than pressure ever did.

Today, choose gentleness in one place where you usually apply force. Notice how your body responds when you soften instead of push.

October 14th: Staying With Yourself in the Quiet

There is a kind of quiet that asks nothing of you. It doesn't demand productivity or response. It simply invites presence.

You may notice how your body responds when things slow down. Breath deepens. Thoughts space out. Sensations become clearer. There is more room to hear what's underneath.

Staying with yourself in this quiet builds trust. You learn that you don't disappear when momentum fades. That you are still here without distraction or effort propping you up.

You are whole in this quiet. Capable. Present.

Today, spend a few moments without distraction. Let yourself stay. Notice what emerges when you don't rush to fill the space.

October 15th: Angels Who Walk Beside You

Some angels don't arrive in dramatic moments. They are simply placed beside you early and continue walking with you through life. They grow alongside you, sharing the same rooms, the same seasons, the same becoming.

This kind of presence feels familiar and steady. The kind that only comes from growing up beside someone, sharing a history no one else fully understands. It shows up in laughter, in shared memories, in the ease of being known without needing to explain yourself. There is comfort in having someone who understands where you come from and chooses to walk with you anyway.

God places certain people in our lives as reminders that we were never meant to do this alone. Their presence doesn't fix everything, but it brightens the path. It brings perspective, warmth, and the quiet reassurance that you are supported.

This love isn't heavy or burdened. It's generous and grounding. It allows you to move through life with more confidence, more joy, and a deeper sense of belonging. It grows richer with time, shaped by shared history and genuine affection.

Today, give thanks for the angel who walks beside you still. Celebrate the companionship, the laughter, and the steady love that continues to shape your life in the best ways.

October 16th: Carrying Grief Gently

Grief has its own rhythm. It doesn't move in straight lines or follow timelines. Sometimes it rests quietly in the background. Other times it rises unexpectedly, even on days that otherwise feel steady.

There is no single way to carry it. No correct pace. No marker that says you should feel lighter, stronger, or further along. Grief can simply exist, taking up the space it needs without explanation or interpretation.

For some, grief changes over time. It may soften, or shift, or settle into the edges of daily life. For others, it remains close, returning in waves or in small, ordinary moments. None of these experiences are wrong. They are just different ways of living alongside what has been lost.

Grief does not have to be resolved in order for life to continue. It can be held with care, acknowledged without being asked to define everything else.

Today, notice what feels present for you. Let that be enough, without needing to name it or move it anywhere else.

October 17th: What Holds

There are seasons when it becomes clear that not everything can be held together by effort or understanding. Plans shift. Certainty loosens. What once felt dependable changes shape.

And yet, something remains.

Not always named. Not always felt in the same way. A quiet presence beneath the noise. A sense of being met, even when answers are missing.

This kind of steadiness doesn't demand belief or clarity. It doesn't require you to feel calm or certain. It simply exists, available in the pauses, in the breath, in the moments when you stop trying to manage what comes next.

You may experience it as faith, or trust, or something harder to define. You may not notice it at all until later.

Today, you might rest in the possibility that you don't have to hold everything on your own. Even briefly, let yourself be held.

October 18th: Letting the Past Be the Past

The past doesn't disappear. It lives in memory, in experience, in the person you became because of it. But it no longer needs to be relived.

You can remember without reopening wounds. You can acknowledge without reentering old patterns. You can honor what was without allowing it to dictate what is.

This isn't forgetting. It's integration. It's recognizing that the past did its work, and that you don't need to keep revisiting it in order to prove you've learned.

You respect who you were without asking that version of you to run your life now.

Today, let one past experience stay where it belongs. Notice the relief that comes from not pulling it into the present moment.

October 19th: Learning to Stay With What You Feel

Some people are rooted not because they are unmoved, but because they feel everything and stay anyway. They notice shifts quickly. They sense undercurrents others miss. Their hearts respond before their minds have time to catch up.

You may recognize this kind of rootedness in yourself now. Not a rigid steadiness, but an emotional one. A capacity to feel joy and ache, excitement and worry, all at once – and still remain present inside your own life. Still choose to stay.

This kind of grounding doesn't come from pushing feelings away. It comes from allowing them. From learning that sensitivity is not something to outgrow, but something to tend. When you stop fighting what you feel, you discover a deeper kind of stability – one built on honesty rather than control.

Being rooted doesn't mean you're unaffected by change. It means you know how to feel deeply without losing yourself. How to let emotion move through you without being swept away.

Today, notice what helps you stay grounded when feelings rise. A breath. A familiar place. A moment of self-compassion. Let yourself be held by what allows you to feel fully and remain steady at the same time.

October 20th: When You No Longer Need Closure

Some things never offer neat endings. Conversations remain unfinished. Losses stay unresolved. Questions linger without answers.

There was a time when you searched for closure as a way to feel safe. As a way to believe the story was complete. But now you know something else is possible.

You can live well without every question answered. You can move forward without tying everything into a bow. Peace does not require resolution.

There is freedom in letting things remain open. In trusting yourself to carry what doesn't make sense without it destabilizing you.

Today, release the need for closure in one place. Notice what happens when you allow peace to arrive anyway.

October 21st: Living With Quiet Confidence

Confidence does not always announce itself. It doesn't always look like boldness or certainty. Often, it looks like calm. Like steadiness. Like no longer needing to explain yourself in rooms where you already know who you are.

You move through your days with a quieter assurance now. You know what matters to you, and you don't feel compelled to defend it. You know when to engage and when to step back. You trust your timing. You trust your instincts. You trust that not every choice needs validation to be right.

This confidence wasn't given to you. It was built slowly, through honesty, self-correction, and the willingness to stay present even when things felt uncomfortable or unclear. It grew each time you listened to yourself instead of overriding what you knew.

Quiet confidence doesn't demand attention. It simply holds you steady.

Today, notice one way this quiet confidence shows up in your life. Let it exist without embellishment or proof. Let it be enough.

October 22nd: No Longer Afraid of the Dark

There was a time when darkness felt threatening. Like something to rush through. Something to distract yourself from. Something that meant you were doing something wrong or missing something important.

But this season has been teaching you something different. Darkness can be quiet. Protective. Honest. It can soften the edges of the world and give your nervous system permission to rest.

You don't lose yourself when the light fades. You don't disappear. Instead, you become more aware of what's already there. Your breath. Your thoughts. Your inner landscape. The parts of you that don't need brightness to exist.

You've learned how to stay with yourself when things are dim. How to listen instead of panic. How to trust that nothing is wrong just because things feel quieter.

Today, notice one moment of darkness – literal or emotional – and allow it to feel safe. Let it hold you rather than threaten you.

October 23rd: The Comfort of Remembering

Memory deepens now, not sharply, but warmly. You remember people, places, and moments that shaped you. Not with urgency or ache, but with tenderness.

There is comfort in remembering this way. Not longing to return, not wishing things were different, but feeling grateful that you lived fully enough to carry these memories with you. That your life has texture. That it has layers.

Remembering doesn't pull you backward. It anchors you. It reminds you of who you've been, what you've survived, and how much love and meaning you've already known.

These memories don't ask to be analyzed or explained. They ask to be felt and honored.

Today, allow yourself to remember something meaningful. Let it bring warmth rather than ache. Let it remind you that your life has been real and deeply lived.

October 24th: When You Trust What Has Endured

So much has changed. Seasons shifted. Roles evolved. Parts of your life fell away or transformed into something unrecognizable.

And yet, some things have stayed.

Your values. Your capacity to feel deeply. Your willingness to choose honesty even when it's uncomfortable. Your ability to pause, reflect, and respond with care instead of reaction.

What has endured deserves your trust. These are not fragile traits. They've been tested by time, by loss, by growth. They've remained because they are true to who you are.

You don't need to question these parts of yourself anymore. You can rely on them.

Today, notice one thing within you that has remained steady through change. Let yourself lean on it. Let it support you.

October 25th: Letting the Body Rest More Deeply

Your body may begin asking for a deeper kind of rest now. Not just sleep, but a fuller letting down. A softening beneath effort and habit.

You might feel slower. Heavier. Less interested in pushing through or keeping pace with expectations that once felt urgent. This is not regression. It's communication.

Your body knows how to prepare for what's ahead. It understands cycles even when your mind resists them.

Deep rest is not something you earn. It's something you allow.

Today, let your body rest more deeply than usual. Cancel if needed. Slow if possible. Lie down without explaining why. Trust that this kind of rest is not wasted – it is necessary.

October 26th: Without Needing to Name It

Some experiences don't need language. They live beneath words, outside explanation. They are felt rather than understood, known rather than articulated. They move through the body without asking to be translated.

You may notice this now in moments that stop you briefly. A feeling that rises without a clear cause. A fullness in your chest. A sudden tenderness. Trying to name these moments can feel like reaching for something that was never meant to be held that way.

Not everything wants to be processed. Some experiences ask only to be felt. When you rush to label them, you move them out of the body and into the mind, where they can lose some of their truth.

There is trust in letting something remain unnamed. It says you don't need to control this experience in order to be okay. You don't need to understand everything to stay present. What is felt is already real.

Today, allow one feeling to exist without naming it. Let it move through you in its own way. Stay with it as sensation, as presence, as truth.

October 27th: The Strength of Being Unseen

Not all strength needs to be visible. Some of the most meaningful work you do happens quietly, without witnesses or applause.

It lives in the choices no one sees. Choosing care when it would be easier to disconnect. Staying sober when no one would know otherwise. Showing up honestly instead of performing. Resting when an old version of you would have pushed through.

This strength doesn't announce itself. It doesn't seek recognition. It simply keeps you aligned with who you are becoming.

You don't need external validation for this work. The fact that you notice it matters.

Today, honor one quiet strength you carry. Let it be enough that you know it's there.

October 28th: When You Stop Measuring Yourself

At some point, comparison loosens its grip. You stop scanning other lives for reference points. You stop measuring your pace against someone else's progress.

Instead, your attention turns inward. Toward how you actually feel inside your own life. Toward what feels honest, sustainable, and real.

This shift brings relief. Space. A sense of coming home to yourself.

You no longer need to ask if you're doing it right. You ask if you're being truthful. If you feel grounded. If you feel like yourself.

Today, release one comparison you've been carrying. Return to your own experience and let it be sufficient.

October 29th: What Warms You When Days Grow Shorter

Warmth doesn't disappear when the days grow shorter. It changes where you find it.

It gathers in small places. In the glow of a lamp before evening has fully settled. In the warmth of a mug between your hands. In familiar movements that make a room feel like home.

You may notice how these small comforts begin to matter more. How you're drawn toward them without thinking. How they quietly hold you as the day softens into night.

Today, pause in one of those moments. Stay there a breath longer than you normally would.

October 30th: When You Trust the Cycle

You've lived long enough now to recognize the rhythm of things. You know that seasons turn. That what fades makes room. That rest is not an ending, but part of the movement.

This knowing softens urgency. You don't panic when energy dips or clarity feels distant. You don't force answers that aren't ready to arrive.

Trusting the cycle allows you to loosen your grip. To stop holding everything together with effort alone.

You understand now that you are not behind. You are where you are meant to be.

Today, trust the cycle you're in. Let yourself move with it rather than against it.

October 31st: Standing at the Edge Without Fear

October closes at the edge of darkness. A night often associated with masks, mystery, and transformation.

But you no longer need to hide behind anything. You've done the quiet work of staying present. Of telling the truth. Of carrying what matters instead of what impresses. You've learned how to stand with yourself even when things feel uncertain or dim.

You are not waiting to become someone else. You are already here. Whole. Aware. Grounded in who you are.

Nothing is asking you to disappear or perform. Nothing is asking you to prove your worth.

Today, stand at the edge of this season without fear. Trust who you are as you step forward, exactly as you are.

November

A slower season of noticing what holds, and letting gratitude arrive.

November 1st: What Still Holds You

The season begins without brightness or urgency. The light is softer now. The world feels quieter, more contained, as if it's gently narrowing your focus. There is less asking for your attention, less pulling you outward.

In this quieter landscape, you may begin to notice what still holds you. The things that haven't fallen away. A routine that steadies your mornings. A relationship that feels reliable rather than demanding. A practice that brings you back into your body when everything else feels uncertain.

These supports don't announce themselves. They don't need to impress. They simply remain. And in their staying, they offer something powerful: continuity.

This is where gratitude begins. Not as celebration or positivity, but as recognition. As seeing clearly what has endured.

Today, notice what is still holding you. Let yourself rest in the steadiness of it without needing to name it as anything more.

November 2nd: Gratitude That Comes From Survival

There is a kind of gratitude that only comes from having lived through something hard. It isn't polished or enthusiastic. It doesn't sparkle. It settles.

You may find yourself grateful for things you once barely noticed. Your breath moving in and out without effort. Your body's ability to recover. Your capacity to stay present with discomfort instead of escaping it.

This gratitude isn't cheerful. It's honest. It carries memory. It knows what it took to arrive here and doesn't forget the cost.

It doesn't demand that you feel lucky or grateful for everything. It simply acknowledges that you're here. That you endured. That something in you kept going when it would have been easier to disappear.

Today, acknowledge one thing you feel grateful for because you survived. Let that gratitude be quiet, grounded, and real.

November 3rd: Noticing What Nourishes You

As things slow, your awareness sharpens. What nourishes you becomes clearer. What drains you is harder to ignore.

You may notice yourself reaching instinctively for warmth. Familiar food. Slower mornings. Deeper rest. There is less interest in excess now, less tolerance for what costs more than it gives.

This isn't indulgence. It's intelligence. Your body remembers what helps it feel safe, supported, and regulated. It remembers what allowed you to keep going when things were difficult.

Nourishment is no longer about reward or permission. It's about care.

Today, choose one nourishing thing intentionally. Let yourself receive it fully, without rushing past it or minimizing its importance.

November 4th: Letting Gratitude Be Simple

Gratitude doesn't need to be elaborate to be real. It doesn't need a list, a ritual, or the right mindset.

Sometimes it lives in ordinary moments. A warm mug held between your hands. A quiet room. The relief of nothing being asked of you right now. The simple fact of being able to pause.

These moments don't look significant from the outside, but they carry weight. They ground you in what is real and present instead of what's missing or unresolved.

Simple gratitude doesn't try to fix anything. It doesn't ask you to feel better. It simply lets you notice what is enough in this moment.

Today, allow yourself to feel grateful for something small and ordinary. Let it matter without dismissing it as insignificant.

November 5th: Thankful for What You Released

Gratitude isn't only about what you have gained. Sometimes it's about what you no longer have to carry.

Old patterns that once felt necessary. Coping mechanisms that helped you survive but no longer serve you. Versions of yourself that worked tirelessly to protect you when you didn't yet know another way.

You don't need to judge who you were. You don't need to regret her. She did important work. She got you here.

But you are not required to keep carrying what once kept you safe.

There is gratitude in recognizing that the weight has shifted. That something has been set down. That effort has softened into choice.

Today, notice one thing you no longer carry. Let gratitude replace obligation. Let relief take the place of duty.

November 6th: The Warmth of Being Understood

There is a particular kind of relief that comes from being understood. Not partially. Not politely. But truly. The kind that lets your shoulders drop because you don't have to translate yourself or defend what you feel.

You may think of a person who listens without interrupting. Who doesn't rush to fix or reframe. Who can hold your truth without needing to reshape it into something more comfortable. Or you may think of a place, a room, a relationship, a space where you are allowed to arrive exactly as you are.

These moments are rare. And because they are rare, they carry weight. They remind you what it feels like to be met instead of managed. Seen instead of assessed.

Being understood is a form of safety. It allows you to rest inside yourself instead of bracing.

Today, hold gratitude for one person or place where you feel understood. Let that warmth spread. Let it remind you that you don't have to do everything alone.

November 7th: Thankful for Staying

There were moments when leaving would have been easier. Turning away. Numbing. Distracting yourself from what hurt instead of staying present with it.

But you stayed.

You stayed with your body when it felt uncomfortable. You stayed with your feelings when they were inconvenient or heavy. You stayed with your life when it would have been easier to disconnect, disappear, or abandon yourself.

Staying didn't always look brave. Sometimes it looked messy. Sometimes it looked quiet. Sometimes it looked like doing the bare minimum to remain present. But it counted.

This kind of staying is not dramatic. It doesn't announce itself. But it changes everything. It builds trust between you and yourself. It creates a foundation you can stand on later.

Today, thank yourself for staying when it would have been easier not to. Let yourself feel the depth of that commitment. It matters more than you may realize.

November 8th: Realizing You Weren't Alone

There is a story many of us carry about surviving hard things through sheer will. About getting through because we were strong enough, disciplined enough, resilient enough on our own.

But when you look more closely, another truth emerges.

You didn't do it alone.

There were hands you leaned on, even briefly. Words that arrived at the right moment. A conversation that shifted something. A place that held you when you couldn't hold yourself. Sometimes the support was obvious. Sometimes it was subtle, almost invisible, but it mattered all the same.

Acknowledging this doesn't take away from your strength. It deepens it. It honors the truth of being human. Of needing each other. Of being shaped not only by effort, but by connection.

Survival is rarely solitary, even when it feels that way at the time.

Today, acknowledge one form of support that helped you through something difficult. Let gratitude soften your chest. Let yourself feel held, even now.

November 9th: Gratitude for the People Who Stayed

Not everyone stayed. Some couldn't. Some weren't able to meet you where you were. Some were meant to walk only part of the way.

But some people did stay.

They stayed when things were complicated. When you weren't easy or upbeat or sure of yourself. When your healing wasn't tidy. When there were no clear answers or quick fixes.

These people didn't rush you. They didn't demand progress or performance. They didn't need you to be different in order to remain present. They stayed because they cared, not because it was comfortable.

That kind of presence leaves a mark. It teaches you what safety feels like. It shows you what connection can be when it's not conditional.

Today, hold gratitude for someone who stayed with you through a difficult season, even in a small or quiet way. Let yourself feel the impact of their presence.

November 10th: Forgiving What You Didn't Know

There were choices you made before you understood yourself. Before you had the language. Before you had the tools. Before you had the support you needed to see clearly.

At the time, you were doing the best you could with what you had. Even if it doesn't look that way in hindsight.

This part of the season invites you to loosen your grip on those moments. To stop replaying them with the added weight of everything you know now. To release the belief that you should have done better when you simply didn't know better.

Forgiving yourself doesn't erase the past. It frees you from living inside it. It allows growth without punishment. Learning without shame.

Compassion does not excuse harm. It acknowledges context. It makes room for truth without cruelty.

Today, offer forgiveness to the version of yourself who didn't know what you know now. Let that forgiveness feel like relief rather than resolution. Let it be gentle.

November 11th: The Body That Carried You

Your body has been with you through every season of your life. Through moments of stress and survival. Through healing, relapse, rebuilding, and learning how to begin again. Long before your mind had language for what was happening, your body was responding. Adjusting. Carrying you forward.

It held tension when there was no other choice. It learned patterns that helped you endure what felt unmanageable at the time. It stayed alert when you needed protection. It kept breathing when you didn't know how to rest. Even when you wanted to disappear, your body stayed.

Gratitude for the body is not about loving every part of it or feeling comfortable in it every day. It's about recognizing its effort. Its loyalty. Its intelligence. It's about acknowledging that this body kept you alive when things were hard, confusing, or painful.

Your body is not something you overcame. It is something that carried you through.

Today, place a hand on your body. Anywhere that feels natural. Offer quiet thanks for the ways it stayed with you when staying was not easy.

November 12th: When You Allow Yourself to Receive

Receiving can feel more vulnerable than giving. Giving keeps you in control. It allows you to stay capable, useful, needed. Receiving asks something else. It asks you to soften. To trust. To let someone else show up for you without immediately balancing the scales.

You may notice how quickly you deflect compliments. How uncomfortable it feels to accept help without returning it right away. How your body tightens when care comes toward you without conditions attached.

This season invites a gentler posture. One where you allow kindness to land instead of brushing it aside. Where you don't rush to prove your worthiness or independence in response to being cared for.

You are allowed to receive without earning it. Without explaining yourself. Without promising to make it even later.

Today, receive one gesture of kindness fully. Let it reach you. Let it stay. Notice what happens in your body when you don't push it away.

November 13th: The Ease of Quiet Care

Some people care for others without making a show of it. They move through the room calmly. They notice what's needed before anyone asks. They tend, adjust, prepare – not out of urgency, but out of presence.

This kind of care doesn't grip tightly. It doesn't manage or control. It trusts the flow of things. It shows up steadily, offering warmth, nourishment, and attention without demanding recognition in return.

There is a softness here that is not passive. It is grounded. Confident. The kind that says, everything is handled, without needing to say much at all. The kind that creates ease simply by being itself.

Softening your grip doesn't mean disengaging. It means staying attentive without strain. It means allowing care to come from steadiness rather than effort.

Today, notice one way care shows up quietly. Through consistency. Through making space. Through small, thoughtful attention that often goes unnoticed. Let yourself appreciate the strength in that kind of gentleness.

November 14th: Thankful for Stepping Away

There are times when staying requires everything you have. And there are times when stepping away is the only way to come back to yourself.

Stepping away doesn't always look dramatic. Sometimes it's quiet. A pause in routine. A decision not to push through. A willingness to place yourself somewhere unfamiliar and let the familiar fall away, even briefly.

Your body often notices first. Shoulders drop without being told. Breath deepens. The constant background hum of responsibility softens just enough for you to hear your own thoughts again. You remember what it feels like to move without urgency, to exist without being needed every second.

This kind of stepping away is not avoidance. It's repair. It's how you remind yourself that you are more than what you produce or hold together.

Today, honor the courage it takes to step away when you need to. Let yourself feel gratitude for choosing restoration without apology.

November 15th: New Places, New Stirring

Being somewhere new changes how you inhabit your body. Your senses sharpen. Your awareness widens. You notice the ground beneath your feet in a way you don't when you're moving through familiar terrain on autopilot.

New landscapes ask something of you. They invite effort and humility at the same time. You climb. You breathe more deliberately. You listen to your body as it navigates unfamiliar ground. You notice beauty even while you're working hard, even while your legs burn or your breath shortens.

There is something deeply grounding about being reminded of both your smallness and your capability at once. About realizing you can meet what's in front of you without needing to conquer it or shrink from it.

Changing your surroundings doesn't fix anything. But it wakes something inside you. A presence. A steadiness. A quiet confidence in your ability to adapt.

Today, notice how being somewhere different awakens parts of you that were resting. Let that awareness travel back with you, wherever you go next.

November 16th: The Depth of New Connections

There is a particular ease that comes with meeting people outside the roles you usually inhabit. No history to carry. No expectations to maintain. No version of yourself you're required to perform.

You meet in motion. In shared effort. In moments of challenge and laughter and quiet presence. These connections form quickly, but they are not rushed. They feel honest because they are rooted in who you are when no one needs anything from you.

There is relief in this kind of connection. You don't have to explain your past or anticipate your future. You are simply here. Breathing. Moving. Participating. Being met as you are in real time.

These moments remind you that connection doesn't always require time or backstory. Sometimes it requires only presence. Openness. A willingness to be seen without armor.

Today, feel gratitude for the connections that meet you right where you are. Let yourself trust their depth without questioning how quickly they formed.

November 17th: Standing at Your Edge

Being away has a way of bringing you to your edge. Physically. Emotionally. Spiritually. Not in a dramatic way, but in quiet moments where you realize you are stretching beyond what feels familiar.

You may find yourself climbing when your legs are tired. Sitting in silence longer than you normally would. Letting yourself not know what comes next without rushing to fill the space. Your edge shows up not as danger, but as invitation.

Standing here teaches humility. It reminds you that growth doesn't come only from mastery or confidence. It comes from willingness. From showing up without needing to be good at something right away. From allowing yourself to be a beginner again.

There is strength in meeting your limits without turning away. In staying present where effort and uncertainty meet.

Today, honor the courage it takes to stand at your edge. Notice how much capacity you already have for staying with what feels new.

November 18th: Carrying the Experience Home

Eventually, you return. To familiar rooms. Familiar rhythms. Familiar responsibilities waiting where you left them.

But something has shifted.

You carry the experience home in ways that don't announce themselves. In how you breathe when tension rises. In how you listen to your body when it asks for rest or movement. In the quiet knowing that you can step away, stretch yourself, and come back more grounded than before.

The journey doesn't end when you unpack your bags. It continues in how you respond to ordinary moments. In how you choose care instead of urgency. In how you trust that what you experienced is still with you, even when the setting has changed.

You don't need to recreate what you felt. You only need to let it inform how you live.

Today, notice what you brought home with you. Let it shape the day gently, without forcing it into form.

November 19th: Choosing What Feels Warm

After connection, effort, and gathering, something inside you starts to ask a quieter question.
Not what's next?
But what feels warm enough to stay with?

You may notice a natural narrowing now. Less desire to explain yourself. Less interest in staying everywhere just to be included. More care around where you place your time, your words, your attention. This isn't withdrawal – it's discernment.

Warmth doesn't come from doing more.
It comes from choosing what soothes your nervous system. What feels safe, familiar, and kind to your body. A small circle. A quiet evening. A conversation that doesn't require effort. Space that lets you exhale instead of perform.

There is nothing wrong with needing less right now. This is how you protect what matters.

Today, choose one thing because it feels warm – not impressive, productive, or expected. Allow yourself to linger there. Notice how your body responds when you choose comfort without apology.

November 20th: Creating Small Rituals of Care

Ritual doesn't need to be elaborate to be meaningful. Often, it's made of small, repeated gestures. Lighting a candle as the light fades. Stretching before bed. Taking a quiet moment before eating. Turning toward yourself with intention.

These small acts signal care. They mark time. They create a sense of steadiness without requiring explanation or performance. They remind your body that it is being tended to.

Ritual grounds you when things feel uncertain. It offers continuity when the world feels in flux. It says, even here, even now, you are held.

You don't need to do everything. You only need to do something consistently enough that your body recognizes it as safety.

Today, create one small ritual of care. Let it anchor you. Let it be simple. Let it be yours.

November 21st: Thankful for a Life That Fits

There may have been a time when you tried to live inside a life that didn't quite fit. When you pushed yourself into shapes that felt too small or too rigid, because you didn't yet know another way. You adjusted. You endured. You told yourself it was fine.

But something shifted.

Now, the life you are living meets you more honestly. It respects your limits instead of testing them. It makes room for your truth instead of asking you to hide it. There is more alignment between who you are and how you move through your days.

This didn't happen by accident. It wasn't luck. It came through courage and choice. Through listening when it would have been easier to ignore yourself. Through walking away from what no longer fit, even when it felt uncertain.

A life that fits doesn't mean a life without challenge. It means a life that doesn't require you to abandon yourself to survive it.

Today, feel gratitude for the life you've shaped. Let it feel like home, even if it's still evolving.

November 22nd: When Gratitude and Grief Coexist

There are days when gratitude feels layered. When it shares space with grief, memory, or longing. When your heart feels full and heavy at the same time.

You may notice this as gatherings approach. Empty chairs. Changed traditions. Relationships that look different than they once did. Versions of yourself who used to show up here in another way.

Nothing is wrong with this complexity.

Gratitude does not require you to erase grief in order to be real. They can sit side by side. They can speak without interrupting each other. One does not cancel the other out.

You are allowed to appreciate what is here while still missing what is not. You are allowed to hold joy and sorrow in the same breath.

Today, allow gratitude and grief to share space. Let them sit at the same table without forcing either one to leave.

November 23rd: Thankful for Those Who Know You

Some people know your surface. They know your roles, your routines, the version of you that shows up easily.

Others know your story.

They know where you've been. They recognize the work it took to arrive here. They understand why certain things matter to you and why certain days feel heavier without needing explanation.

These people don't rush your healing or simplify your experience. They don't need you to perform gratitude or strength. They meet you with care because they know the context of your life.

This kind of knowing is rare. It's built through time, honesty, and shared vulnerability. And it is a gift.

Today, hold gratitude for someone who knows your story and still chooses to meet you with kindness. Let yourself feel how held that kind of understanding can be.

November 24th: Letting the Day Be

There can be pressure around certain days to feel a particular way. To be joyful. To be present. To be grateful on demand. As if emotion should rise on cue.

But truth does not bend to expectation.

You are allowed to let the day be what it is. Messy or quiet. Full or tender. Ordinary or heavy. You don't need to manage your feelings or rush yourself into the "right" experience.

Gratitude grows best when it is honest, not forced. When it arises naturally instead of being required.

Letting the day be what it is creates space for something real to emerge. Even if that something is simply neutrality. Or rest.

Today, allow the day to unfold without insisting it feel a certain way. Let yourself meet it honestly, moment by moment.

November 25th: Thankful for What Didn't Break You

There were moments that could have broken you. Seasons that tested your limits. Experiences that demanded more than you thought you had to give. And yet, you are still here.

This gratitude is not about minimizing what you went through or pretending it made you stronger in some neat, inspirational way. It's about acknowledging endurance. The capacity to stay. The willingness to keep choosing life even when it felt heavy or uncertain.

Along the way, you may have encountered people who showed you what staying looks like. Not by fixing anything for you, but by embodying steadiness, presence, and care. People whose way of moving through the world quietly reminded you that healing was possible, even when you weren't sure how to begin.

You survived not because it was easy, but because something in you kept going. Sometimes quietly. Sometimes imperfectly. Often supported by what you witnessed in others. Strength reflected back to you before you fully recognized it as your own.

Today, acknowledge something you survived. Let gratitude honor your strength and the influences that helped shape it, without needing to explain or elevate them. Simply recognize that you are still standing, and that you did not arrive here alone.

November 26th: When You Choose Simplicity

There comes a moment when your body begins to ask for less. Not because something is wrong, but because it has been paying attention long enough to know what it can reasonably carry.

You may notice this request in subtle ways. A reluctance to over-explain yourself. A desire for fewer plans, fewer conversations, fewer obligations that require you to be "on." A longing for spaces where you don't have to perform, prove, or manage anyone else's experience.

This pull toward simplicity isn't avoidance. It's discernment. A quiet wisdom that recognizes your energy as precious and finite. You are no longer interested in spending it everywhere just because you can.

Simplicity doesn't mean withdrawing from life or giving everything up. It means choosing with care. Letting what matters stay close, and allowing the rest to soften at the edges without guilt.

Today, choose one small way to simplify. Notice how your body responds when you do. Pay attention to the relief that comes from choosing less, on purpose.

November 27th: Gratitude for the Quiet After

There is a particular kind of quiet that comes after fullness. After effort. After connection. After being present in a way that asked something of you.

The noise fades. The body exhales. The constant need to respond or hold things together loosens its grip. You may notice how the space around you feels different once there is nothing left to manage.

In this quiet, your nervous system unwinds. Breath deepens without instruction. You return to yourself without needing to earn it or explain why you need it.

This is not emptiness. It is integration. The moment where experience settles into the body and becomes something you can carry forward with more ease.

Today, notice the quiet that follows something full. Let it restore you. Let it be enough without filling it.

November 28th: What Remains With You

Not everything you live through is meant to stay with you. Some experiences pass through, doing their work, then releasing their hold.

But some things remain.

A steadier relationship with your body. A clearer understanding of your limits. A softer, more honest way of speaking to yourself when things feel hard. These aren't lessons you force yourself to remember. They travel with you naturally, shaping how you move, choose, and respond.

What you carry forward now feels supportive rather than heavy. It doesn't demand attention. It simply shows up when you need it.

You don't have to keep everything. Only what feels true.

Today, notice one thing you're grateful to carry with you. Let it feel like support rather than responsibility.

November 29th: Trusting the Slowing Down

There are times when your body asks for a slower pace, even when your mind resists. More pauses. More rest. Fewer demands competing for your attention.

You may feel the familiar urge to push through. To stay productive. To prove you can keep going, even when you're tired. But this slowing is not a failure of will. It's information.

Slowing down is an act of listening. It teaches you how to move with intention instead of urgency. How to conserve energy instead of spending it reactively. How to notice what actually matters when the noise quiets.

Nothing essential is lost when you slow down. Often, it's when you finally notice what's been there all along.

Today, allow yourself to move more slowly than usual. Trust that this pace is not holding you back. It is bringing you closer to yourself.

November 30th: Carrying Gratitude Gently

Gratitude does not always arrive as joy or enthusiasm. Sometimes it lives quietly in the body. In the steadiness of breath. In the simple knowing of what has held you before and will likely hold you again.

You don't need to feel bright or optimistic to be grateful. Gratitude can coexist with heaviness, uncertainty, and fatigue. It doesn't demand performance or expression.

At this point, gratitude becomes something you carry rather than something you display. It grounds you. It steadies you. It reminds you of continuity without asking you to feel any particular way.

You don't have to hold it tightly. You don't have to name it perfectly.

Today, let gratitude live gently inside you. Trust that it will meet you again when you need it, without effort or demand.

December

*Releasing what you cannot carry,
and trusting what carries you.*

December 1st: Entering the Quiet

This month begins without announcement. No urgency. No demand to arrive as anything other than you are. The world has pulled inward, and the light sits lower in the sky, as if listening.

You may feel this shift before you name it. A longer pause between thoughts. A slower rhythm in your body. A sense that you don't need to move yet. After months of responding, adjusting, and letting go, there is relief in not being asked to expand.

This quiet is not absence. It is space. Space for what you lived to settle. Space where nothing needs fixing or improving. Space where effort can finally rest.

You are not behind. You are not missing anything. You are arriving exactly where you are meant to be.

Today, allow yourself to enter the quiet without filling it. Notice what it feels like to begin from stillness rather than momentum.

December 2nd: What Teaches You to Slow Down

Some beings teach you to slow down simply by how they move through the world.
Unhurried. Attentive. Guided by rhythm instead of urgency.

Their presence settles the body. Breathing softens. Shoulders drop. The nervous system remembers it doesn't have to stay alert or braced. Around them, slowing down isn't a decision – it happens naturally. You stop pushing. You stop rushing toward what's next.

There is a kind of grace here that isn't performed or explained. It's lived. It knows when to rest, when to stay close, when the day has asked enough. It reminds you that nothing needs fixing or proving in this moment.

From this place, rest doesn't have to be earned. Love can be steady and uncomplicated. Connection can be quiet and complete.

Today, let what softens you set the pace. Move more slowly. Stay longer. Rest without apology. Let presence be enough.

December 3rd: Letting the Year Settle in Your Body

You have lived a lot this year. Even if it didn't look dramatic from the outside, your body knows. It remembers the stress, the healing, the decisions, the moments you stayed when it was hard.

As the year winds down, your body begins to gather these experiences and make sense of them in its own way. Not through thinking, but through sensation. Through the need for rest. Through emotion that surfaces without a clear story attached.

You don't need to review or assess everything that happened. Your body is already doing the work of sorting what stays and what can be released.

This settling takes time. It can't be rushed.

Today, check in with your body. Notice what feels heavy, what feels tired, what feels complete. Let the year settle without asking it to explain itself.

December 4th: When You Stop Pushing for Closure

As the year winds down, there can be a subtle pressure to make sense of everything. To tie loose ends. To understand what was painful. To decide what it all meant.

But not everything is ready to be concluded.

Some experiences are still settling beneath the surface. Some lessons are integrating quietly, without language. Some questions are meant to stay open a while longer.

You do not need resolution in order to move forward. You do not need answers in order to be at peace.

There is relief in letting things remain unfinished without believing that *you* are incomplete.

Today, notice where you can stop pushing for clarity. Let yourself rest inside what hasn't resolved yet.

December 5th: Resting Without Anticipation

Rest can be elusive when part of you is already leaning ahead. Planning. Preparing. Bracing for what comes next.

But this season offers another kind of rest. Not rest that exists to refuel productivity. Not rest with an agenda attached. Just rest.

This is rest that allows your nervous system to soften. Rest that reminds you you're allowed to pause without explanation or outcome.

You don't need to make this rest useful. You don't need to do it well.

You are allowed to stop.

Today, rest without anticipating what comes after. Let the pause be complete on its own.

December 6th: Letting the Days Be Smaller

The days don't ask for much right now. Light comes and goes quietly. Time feels less dramatic, more contained.
You may notice a natural desire for smaller plans. Shorter conversations. Simpler meals. Earlier nights.

This shrinking isn't loss. It's focus.
When the world narrows, what matters becomes clearer. You don't need to stretch yourself thin to feel alive. You don't need constant stimulation to feel connected.

There is relief in letting the days be smaller.
In doing fewer things with more presence.
In allowing life to fit comfortably in your hands instead of spilling over.

Today, let one part of your day be intentionally small. Notice how steadiness grows when you stop reaching for more.

December 7th: Seeing With New Eyes

There comes a time in life when something quietly shifts.

You look around and realize that no one actually has this figured out. Everyone is living their life for the very first time, learning as they go, doing the best they can with what they've been given. The certainty you once expected from others softens. A different kind of understanding comes into view.

You begin to see people with new eyes. Not as finished versions of who they should be, but as human beings still becoming. Still practicing. Still carrying their own fears, hopes, and unhealed places.

This realization can be especially tender when it turns toward your parents. The people you once believed were supposed to know everything. You begin to see them not only as caregivers or authority figures, but as people who were also figuring it out in real time. Loving without a manual. Making choices without guarantees. Carrying their own stories into the way they showed up for you.

This perspective doesn't erase the hard moments. But it can soften the edges around them. It invites compassion where there may have once been judgment. It creates space for grace, for yourself and for those who came before you.

Today, notice one place where you can widen your view. Where seeing someone as human, learning, and imperfect allows your heart to soften just a little.

December 8th: When Quiet Feels Like Company

There is a kind of quiet now that doesn't feel empty. It feels companionable.
Like sitting beside someone who doesn't need conversation.
Like being alone without feeling lonely.

You may notice moments where silence feels supportive rather than awkward. Where you don't reach for noise or distraction out of habit. Where being with yourself feels enough.

This is a sign of trust.
Trust in your own presence.
Trust that you don't disappear when things get quiet.

Today, spend a few moments in silence without filling it. Let the quiet keep you company instead of something you have to manage.

December 9th: Releasing the Need to Finish Strong

There is a familiar pressure near the end of things to push harder. To rally. To prove something with a final burst of effort. As if the worth of the whole is determined by how forcefully you cross the finish line.

But this season asks for something else.

It asks you to notice how much you've already given. How many times you showed up when you were tired. How often you stayed when it would have been easier to disengage. Strength has already been expressed. It doesn't need a final performance.

Finishing strong is not the same as finishing honestly. Sometimes honesty looks like slowing down. Letting the last steps be quieter. Allowing yourself to arrive without spectacle or exhaustion.

You don't need to sprint to be worthy of rest. You don't need to prove the year mattered by ending it breathless.

Today, release the need to finish strong. Let yourself finish true.

December 10th: Carrying Warmth Into the Dark

As darkness arrives earlier, warmth becomes intentional.
It's created, not assumed.
A lamp turned on. A blanket pulled closer. A choice to stay present instead of retreating inward.

This warmth is not about avoiding darkness.
It's about learning how to live well inside it.
How to tend yourself when light is limited.

You are learning how to be your own source of steadiness.
How to bring care into spaces that once felt cold or uncertain.

Today, notice one way you create warmth for yourself. Let it matter. Let it be enough for this moment.

December 11th: When the Body Asks You to Slow

There is a deeper slowing now. Not the kind that feels optional, but the kind your body asks for quietly and persistently. You may notice it in heavier limbs. Longer pauses between thoughts. A resistance to rushing that feels physical, not philosophical.

This is not laziness. It's not disengagement.
It's your system recalibrating after a year of holding, responding, adapting.

The body does this when it finally trusts that it doesn't have to stay alert anymore. When it believes that rest will not be taken away the moment it arrives.
Slowing further is a sign of safety.

You don't need to argue with this pace or explain it away.
You don't need to justify why you're tired.
You're allowed to listen.

Today, notice where your body is asking for less. Let that request guide you, even if your mind wants to keep pushing.

December 12th: The Tenderness Beneath the Fatigue

Fatigue this time of year often carries emotion beneath it.
Not just tiredness, but tenderness.
A softness that comes from everything you've carried, everything you've navigated, everything you didn't get to set down until now.

You may feel more easily moved. More sensitive to tone, memory, or absence.
You may feel close to tears without a clear reason why.

Nothing is wrong.
This tenderness is what happens when defenses lower.
When you no longer need to stay braced.
When your heart realizes it can come closer to the surface.

There is wisdom in this softness.
It means you're not hardened by what you've lived.
It means you're still open.

Today, treat your tenderness with care instead of control. Let it exist without trying to toughen yourself against it.

December 13th: Listening to the Body's Wisdom

Before the mind can summarize a year, the body speaks.
It speaks through ache and ease.
Through what feels complete and what still feels tender.
Through what no longer tightens when you think about it, and what still does.

You don't need to review the year intellectually.
You don't need to extract lessons or craft meaning.
Your body already knows what mattered.

It knows where you grew.
It knows where you were stretched.
It knows what changed you quietly and what exhausted you deeply.

Listening to the body now is an act of respect.
It's how you honor what you lived without forcing it into language too soon.

Today, notice what your body remembers about this year. Let it communicate without translating it into conclusions.

December 14th: When Stillness Feels Honest

Stillness can feel confronting in a world that values motion.
But this stillness feels different.
It feels honest.

There is less pretending now.
Less striving to appear okay, productive, or resolved.
Stillness strips things down to what's actually here.

You may notice that when you stop moving, something true rises.
Not necessarily something dramatic.
Often something simple.
A clear no.
A quiet yes.
A feeling you've been carrying without naming.

Stillness doesn't demand action.
It offers clarity without pressure.

Today, allow yourself a stretch of real stillness. Let it show you what has been waiting beneath the noise.

December 15th: Standing With Yourself at the End

There comes a moment in December when effort naturally loosens. Not because everything is finished, but because something inside you knows it's time to stop pushing.

You may feel less driven to plan or repair. Less interested in explaining yourself. More willing to let things remain unresolved.

This isn't quitting. It's integration.

Standing with yourself at the end of effort means trusting that you did enough. That what mattered was tended to. That what didn't resolve does not need to be forced into meaning.

You are allowed to arrive here without polish. Without conclusions. Without a summary.

Today, stand with yourself exactly where you are. Let effort rest. Let presence take its place.

December 16th: Letting the Year Be

There is a subtle shift when you realize you are no longer trying to fix what this year was. You stop replaying moments to see how they could have gone differently. You stop asking yourself if you handled things the right way. You stop scanning for mistakes that need correcting.

This is not because everything turned out perfectly. It's because you've reached a point of honesty where you can say: this is what happened, and I lived it.

Fixing is often a form of control. A way of believing that if you just think hard enough, you can undo what hurt or smooth what was rough. But now, the need to fix softens. What's left is acceptance without resignation.

You are allowed to let the year be what it was. Complex. Imperfect. Meaningful. Hard. Real.

Today, notice where you're no longer trying to fix the past. Let that space feel like relief instead of loss.

December 17th: The Relief of Not Explaining Yourself

There is a relief that comes when you realize you don't owe explanations anymore. Not for how you feel. Not for why you're tired. Not for the choices you've made to protect your peace.

You may notice this most in conversations you no longer engage in. Justifications you don't offer. Stories you don't retell to make yourself more understandable or acceptable.

This isn't withdrawal. It's trust.

Trust that the people who matter don't need convincing. Trust that your inner knowing is enough. Trust that your life doesn't need to make sense to everyone in order to be valid.

Silence becomes spacious instead of awkward. Boundaries feel calmer instead of defensive.

Today, allow one decision or feeling to exist without explanation. Notice how steady that feels in your body.

December 18th: When the Body Closes the Year

The body closes the year before the calendar does.

You may feel it in deeper sleep. Or heavier exhaustion. Or a desire to cocoon, to stay close, to pull inward without guilt. Your system knows something is ending, even if nothing external has changed yet.

This closing is not dramatic. It's cellular. The body gathering itself after months of responding, adjusting, and holding.

You might feel less interested in new input. Less willing to take on more. Less available for emotional labor that once felt manageable.

This is not failure. It's completion beginning to take shape.

Today, notice how your body is preparing to close this year. Let it lead instead of overriding it.

December 19th: Letting Enough Be Enough

Near the end of the year, it's easy to start tallying. Measuring progress. Assessing growth. Asking whether you did enough.

But another truth is available now.

What you did was enough because it was real. Because you stayed inside your life instead of escaping it. Because you met what came with the capacity you had at the time.

Enough does not mean easy. It does not mean flawless. It means honest.

You don't need to inflate accomplishments or extract lessons to justify this year. Its worth is not up for debate.

Today, let what was be enough. Allow that truth to settle without argument.

December 20th: Standing at the Edge

You are nearing the edge of the year now, but nothing is asking you to cross yet. There is no demand for clarity, intention, or resolve.

Standing here, you may feel both an ending and an opening at the same time. Something closing. Something quietly forming. Neither needs your immediate attention.

Urgency fades when you trust timing. When you trust that what's meant to arrive will not pass you by. When you trust that rest is not wasted.

You don't need to step forward yet.

Today, pause at the edge without reaching ahead. Let yourself remain exactly where you are.

December 21st: The Longest Night

Today holds the longest night of the year. Darkness stretches fully, unapologetically, before anything begins to turn back toward the light.

This darkness is not a threat. It is a pause. A still point. A moment where nothing more is asked of you except to be here.

You may feel the weight of the year more clearly now. What you carried. What you lost. What changed you. There is no need to rush past this heaviness or reframe it into something hopeful. This night allows depth without explanation.

The longest night exists so the light doesn't have to be forced. It returns because it is time, not because you made it happen.

Today, honor the darkness without fear. Let yourself rest in it, trusting that nothing has gone wrong simply because things feel still.

December 22nd: When Rest Becomes Permission

There is a kind of rest that comes only when you stop asking if it's allowed.

Not rest earned through productivity. Not rest justified by exhaustion. But rest that exists because your body and spirit have reached the end of a long cycle.

You may notice how deeply you want to pull inward now. Fewer words. Fewer plans. More stillness. This is not withdrawal. It is restoration beginning to take shape.

Permission doesn't arrive from outside. It comes when you decide you no longer need to prove anything.

Today, allow rest without negotiating with it. Let it be given rather than taken.

December 23rd: Carrying the Year in Your Body

Before you reflect on the year with your mind, your body remembers it first.

It remembers the tension it held. The moments it braced. The times it softened. The ways it learned new rhythms in response to what life asked of you.

You may feel this in fatigue that has no clear source. Or in a heaviness that doesn't need fixing. Or in a tenderness that surfaces unexpectedly.

Your body is not asking for analysis. It is asking for acknowledgment.

Today, place a hand somewhere on your body and recognize the year it carried. Let gratitude be felt, not spoken.

December 24th: Letting the Day Be Tender

There is often pressure around this day. Pressure to feel connected. Joyful. Nostalgic. Present in the "right" way.

But tenderness doesn't follow schedules.

You may feel closeness and distance at the same time. Gratitude and grief sharing space. Comfort brushing up against longing. None of this means you're doing the day wrong.

Tenderness is honesty without armor. It's letting the moment be what it is instead of insisting it be something else.

Today, allow the day to be tender. Meet it gently. You don't have to hold everything together.

December 25th: The Quiet Meaning of Enough

This day does not need to be loud to be holy.
Its meaning has never depended on spectacle or abundance.
It began in stillness. In a body. In a world that did not make room, and yet was changed forever.

Meaning may arrive now the same way. In a quiet morning. In breath before conversation. In the simple fact of being here. Loved. Held. Counted, even if nothing looks the way you imagined it would.

Enough is not measured by what is present or absent, gathered or missing. It is revealed when striving loosens its grip. When you remember that worth was never something you were meant to earn.

God did not wait for the world to be ready.
Love entered as it was.
Vulnerable. Ordinary. Small.

You do not need to recreate the past. You do not need to manufacture joy or force gratitude. You only need to receive what has already been given.

Today, let yourself be enough – not because you feel complete, but because you are already loved. Let that truth be the gift you receive. And the quiet grace you carry forward.

December 26th: After the Gathering

There is a particular feeling that arrives after something has passed. The quiet that follows effort. The exhale after holding space. The stillness that settles once there is nothing left to prepare for or respond to.

Your body often feels this before your mind does. A heaviness. A tenderness. A desire to withdraw slightly, not out of sadness, but out of completion.

This space is not emptiness. It is integration. The place where experience moves from something you lived into something that becomes part of you.

Today, honor the quiet after. Let yourself land without rushing to fill the space with plans or meaning.

December 27th: Letting the Year Soften

The year begins to loosen its grip now. Not dramatically. Gently.

You may notice the urgency fading. The pressure to keep up, keep proving, keep pushing slowly dissolving. What remains feels quieter and more honest.

This softening does not mean the year didn't matter. It means it no longer needs to be held so tightly.

Some things are ready to be remembered with less charge. Others are ready to be released without ceremony.

Today, allow the year to soften. Notice what no longer needs your effort to hold.

December 28th: When Reflection Happens Naturally

Reflection doesn't need to be forced. It doesn't require a list, a summary, or a verdict.

Often, it arrives sideways. In moments of stillness. In a memory that surfaces without invitation. In the quiet realization that something feels different now, even if you can't name exactly how.

This kind of reflection is bodily. Emotional. Subtle.

You don't need to evaluate the year. You don't need to decide whether it was good or bad, successful or wasted.

Today, notice what reflects itself naturally. Trust what arises without interrogating it.

December 29th: Letting It Be Unfinished

Not everything that happened this year will make sense. Not everything will fit into a clean narrative of growth or purpose.

Some moments were simply hard. Some losses remain unresolved. Some changes happened without explanation or closure.

You are allowed to stop trying to organize your life into something understandable.

Meaning does not require clarity. Healing does not require answers.

Today, release the need to make sense of everything. Let what is unfinished remain unfinished.

December 30th: Standing at the Threshold

You are close to the edge now. Not an ending exactly. Not a beginning yet. A threshold.

There is no rush here. No requirement to cross with intention or insight or readiness.

You are allowed to stand in this in-between space without declaring what comes next. Without setting goals. Without promising transformation.

Thresholds are meant to be felt, not managed.

Today, stand where you are without reaching ahead. Trust that movement will come when it's time.

December 31st: Carrying Only What Is True

The year does not ask you for a summary as it closes. It does not require a verdict or a lesson learned, and it does not demand that you explain what this year was or who you became because of it. It simply ends.

In that ending, there is a reckoning – not with what you accomplished, but with what stayed. With what endured when things fell apart. With what remained when the noise faded.

You may feel the weight of everything you lived – the joy that surprised you, the grief that never fully left, the ways you showed up when you didn't think you could, and the moments you chose to return. All of it belongs to the year you are leaving behind. But you do not have to carry all of it forward.

There are parts of this year that shaped you and can now be set down – the vigilance, the self-blame, the pressure to hold everything together alone. You are allowed to leave those here. What you carry forward is truer: the steadiness you built slowly, the honesty you practiced even when it cost you comfort, the way you learned to stay with yourself instead of abandoning your own body or heart.

As the year closes, let yourself feel the tenderness of this moment – the gratitude, the ache, the relief of having lived another year honestly. Tonight, choose one thing to carry with you, one truth that feels like home in your body. Let it be enough, and let the rest stay here.

Closing

If you've reached this page, it doesn't mean you're finished.

This book was never meant to be completed in a straight line, or all at once, or only once. It was meant to be returned to. Opened on quiet mornings. Reached for on heavy days. Left on a nightstand, a kitchen counter, the passenger seat.

You may have read some pages slowly and others not at all. You may have skipped ahead, lingered, or set the book down for weeks. All of that is part of the rhythm.

What matters is not how much you read, but that you felt held while you were here.

If something in these pages met you where you were, let that be enough.

If nothing landed today, trust that another day it might. You can begin again whenever you need to.

www.ingramcontent.com/pod-product-compliance
Lightning Source LLC
LaVergne TN
LVHW091700070526
838199LV00050B/2225